T0224847

# Payara Micro Revealed

## Cloud-Native Application
## Development with Java

David R. Heffelfinger

Apress®

*Payara Micro Revealed: Cloud-Native Application Development with Java*

David R. Heffelfinger
Fairfax, VA, USA

ISBN-13 (pbk): 978-1-4842-8160-4          ISBN-13 (electronic): 978-1-4842-8161-1
https://doi.org/10.1007/978-1-4842-8161-1

Copyright © 2022 by David R. Heffelfinger

This work is subject to copyright. All rights are reserved by the Publisher, whether the whole or part of the material is concerned, specifically the rights of translation, reprinting, reuse of illustrations, recitation, broadcasting, reproduction on microfilms or in any other physical way, and transmission or information storage and retrieval, electronic adaptation, computer software, or by similar or dissimilar methodology now known or hereafter developed.

Trademarked names, logos, and images may appear in this book. Rather than use a trademark symbol with every occurrence of a trademarked name, logo, or image we use the names, logos, and images only in an editorial fashion and to the benefit of the trademark owner, with no intention of infringement of the trademark.

The use in this publication of trade names, trademarks, service marks, and similar terms, even if they are not identified as such, is not to be taken as an expression of opinion as to whether or not they are subject to proprietary rights.

While the advice and information in this book are believed to be true and accurate at the date of publication, neither the authors nor the editors nor the publisher can accept any legal responsibility for any errors or omissions that may be made. The publisher makes no warranty, express or implied, with respect to the material contained herein.

Managing Director, Apress Media LLC: Welmoed Spahr
Acquisitions Editor: Jonathan Gennick
Development Editor: Laura Berendson
Coordinating Editor: Jill Balzano

Cover image designed by Freepik (www.freepik.com)

Distributed to the book trade worldwide by Springer Science+Business Media LLC, 1 New York Plaza, Suite 4600, New York, NY 10004. Phone 1-800-SPRINGER, fax (201) 348-4505, e-mail orders-ny@springer-sbm. com, or visit www.springeronline.com. Apress Media, LLC is a California LLC and the sole member (owner) is Springer Science + Business Media Finance Inc (SSBM Finance Inc). SSBM Finance Inc is a **Delaware** corporation.

For information on translations, please e-mail booktranslations@springernature.com; for reprint, paperback, or audio rights, please e-mail bookpermissions@springernature.com.

Apress titles may be purchased in bulk for academic, corporate, or promotional use. eBook versions and licenses are also available for most titles. For more information, reference our Print and eBook Bulk Sales web page at http://www.apress.com/bulk-sales.

Any source code or other supplementary material referenced by the author in this book is available to readers on GitHub.

Printed on acid-free paper

# Table of Contents

# About the Author

**David Heffelfinger** is an independent consultant at Ensode Technology, LLC (`www.ensode.com`). David has authored several books on Jakarta EE and related technologies. He is a frequent speaker at tech conferences such as JavaOne and Oracle Code One. David has served in the JavaOne content committee on multiple occasions. He was named one of 39 Java leaders and experts to follow on Twitter, where you can find him under the handle @ensode.

# About the Technical Reviewer

**Andres Sacco** has been working as a developer since 2007 in different languages including Java, PHP, NodeJs, and Android. Most of his background is in Java and the libraries or frameworks associated with this language, for example, Spring, Hibernate, JSF, and Quarkus. In most of the companies that he worked for, he researched new technologies in order to improve the performance, stability, and quality of the applications of each company.

# Acknowledgments

I would like to thank the Apress editorial team, particularly Jonathan Gennick and Jill Balzano for their guidance and support.

I would also like to thank Andres Sacco, the technical reviewer, for his invaluable feedback.

Additionally, I would like to thank Rudy De Busscher, Product Manager at Payara Services Ltd, for his assistance.

Finally, I would like to thank my wife and daughters for putting up with the long hours of work that kept me away from the family.

# CHAPTER 1

# Jakarta EE, MicroProfile, Payara, and the Cloud

Payara is a Jakarta EE and MicroProfile–compliant runtime; both of these are specifications dictating standards for server-side and cloud-based applications. In this chapter, we will provide a brief history of server-side Java and Payara to give some context on how we got to where we are today.

## Brief Server-Side Java History

The Java language was released to the world by Sun Microsystems in 1995, and it took the world by storm. In the beginning, the killer feature of Java was Java applets, a technology that allowed rich "desktop-like" applications to run inside web browsers.

Sun Microsystems started expanding the Java language beyond desktop applications, splitting the language into three editions in 1999; the three editions were called J2SE (Java 2 Standard Edition), J2ME (Java 2, Micro Edition), and J2EE (Java 2, Enterprise Edition).

The introduction of J2EE back in 1999 was a huge success. Sun Microsystems created a standard that other vendors could implement, demand for J2EE soared, and a large number of vendors created products implementing the standard. Some of those products still exist today, like Red Hat JBoss, Oracle WebLogic, and IBM WebSphere application servers.

## J2EE

J2EE was a huge success; it provided APIs that were previously part of the Java language, such as servlets, used to generate markup (typically HTML) on the server, to be

1

© David R. Heffelfinger 2022
D. R. Heffelfinger, *Payara Micro Revealed*, https://doi.org/10.1007/978-1-4842-8161-1_1

displayed on the client (typically a web browser). J2EE introduced several new APIs and technologies that became very popular, such as Java Server Pages (JSP), which made it easier to generate markup server side than it was possible with servlets, and Enterprise Java Beans (EJB), which automated a lot of enterprise requirements such as transactions and security.

J2EE was such a huge success that, even though competing server-side Java technologies emerged, such as the popular Spring Framework, the term J2EE became a generic term meaning "server-side Java." It wasn't uncommon for job postings to request J2EE expertise, where the position in question required minimal, if any, actual J2EE knowledge, instead focusing on competing Java technologies.

To this day, it isn't that uncommon to find the term J2EE in job postings and even in informal conversations related to server-side Java, even though J2EE has been obsolete for several years, superseded by Java EE way back in 2006.

# Java EE

Although widely popular, J2EE gained a reputation for being complex and difficult to use. As such, several competing technologies started popping up, claiming to provide equivalent functionality to J2EE, while being easier to work with. Some prominent J2EE competitors at the time included Ruby on Rails and the Spring Framework.

As a response to these competing technologies, Sun Microsystems introduced Java EE (Java, Enterprise Edition) in 2006. Java EE introduced the heavy use of annotations for application configuration, greatly simplifying the task of configuring and developing server-side Java applications.

---

Some time after the release of Java EE, Oracle Corporation acquired Sun Microsystems; as such, Oracle became the new steward of the Java language and, by extension, of Java EE.

---

Java EE applications, like J2EE before it, were originally meant to be deployed to an application server, which is a piece of enterprise software that takes care of a lot of the "plumbing" of the application, freeing application developers to focus on implementing business logic. These application servers tend to be resource heavy, needing large amounts of computing resources such as RAM and CPU.

At some point after the release of Java EE, cloud-based deployments started gaining popularity, which led in no small part by the popularity of Amazon Web Services. Instead of hosting servers on-site, companies could now rent computing power from cloud providers, freeing these companies from having to procure and maintain their own servers. These cloud providers charge their customers by the resources (CPU, memory, bandwidth, etc.) they actually use, in many cases greatly reducing costs for their customers.

By their very nature, applications developed to the cloud should not be resource intensive. With the rise in popularity of cloud deployments, traditional Java EE applications, with their monolithic, resource-heavy application servers, started losing popularity. Java EE implementation vendors responded by developing lightweight versions of their application servers, better suited for cloud deployments.

In addition to developing lightweight versions of their offerings, a number of application server vendors started cooperating to create a new standard, tailored specifically for cloud deployments; the result of this effort was the birth of MicroProfile. MicroProfile 1.0 was officially released in San Francisco during the JavaOne conference in 2016.

# MicroProfile

Just like Java EE before it, MicroProfile is a specification (a piece of paper, if you will), with multiple implementations. MicroProfile provides specifications for APIs commonly needed when deploying to the cloud, such as application configuration, health checks, request tracing, metrics, fault tolerance, documentation, and security.

MicroProfile also shares some APIs with Jakarta EE (the successor to Java EE; see the next section), namely, Jakarta RESTful Web Services (formerly known as JAX-RS), Jakarta Contexts and Dependency Injection (CDI), Jakarta JSON Binding, and Jakarta JSON Processing.

Jakarta RESTful Web Services, unsurprisingly, is an API used to develop RESTful web services. Developing RESTful web services with this API is very simple, with most of the work done by adding a few simple annotations.

Jakarta Contexts and Dependency Injection (CDI) is an API that facilitates injecting dependencies into application code. It also provides scopes (such as request, session, application, and so on) to Java Beans managed by CDI.

Jakarta JSON Binding and JSON Processing APIs are used when working with data in JavaScript Object Notation (JSON) format, which is by far the most common format used when working with microservices and web services. Jakarta JSON Binding is a high-level API that does a lot of work behind the scenes, while Jakarta JSON Processing is a lower-level API that provides more control for application developers.

# Jakarta EE

In 2017, Oracle donated Java EE to the Eclipse Foundation; at this point in time, the technology was renamed to Jakarta EE. With the donation to the Eclipse Foundation, there was no longer any single entity controlling the standard; instead, several equal partner companies contribute equally to it; even individual contributors not affiliated with any Jakarta EE vendor can join the foundation and contribute to the standard.

Although the lines have blurred in recent years, Jakarta EE is primarily thought of as a specification for traditional on-site application deployments using monolithic application servers. MicroProfile, on the other hand, is thought of as a specification meant for lightweight cloud deployments.

Although cloud deployment has become very popular in recent years, it isn't a panacea; it doesn't always make sense to develop applications for the cloud.

Additionally, there are several applications developed in the days before cloud deployments became popular, which would be too costly or impractical to migrate to a new architecture.

Most popular Jakarta EE implementations provide a lightweight version of their offerings (i.e., Payara Micro), making the task of migrating Jakarta EE applications to the cloud easier and even easing the task of developing new Jakarta EE–compliant applications specifically for the cloud.

# Payara

Payara started as a fork of GlassFish application server. For readers not aware, GlassFish used to be an open source Java EE implementation from Oracle (and Sun Microsystems before them). GlassFish used to be the Java EE reference implementation. For many years, commercial support was available for GlassFish; however, at some point, support was dropped, although GlassFish was still freely available for download.

Many organizations require support contracts for any software they utilize in production; GlassFish commercial support being dropped left many companies scrambling looking for a replacement.

C2B2 Consulting, a UK-based company, saw an opportunity and created Payara as a fork of GlassFish. Being based on GlassFish, it was seamless to transition applications developed for GlassFish to Payara.

C2B2 Consulting has been maintaining Payara and adding additional features not originally available in GlassFish, including splitting Payara into two editions: "Payara Server," which is a traditional Jakarta EE application server, and "Payara Micro," which is meant to be deployed to a cloud environment.

Payara is fully open source; under the Common Development and Distribution License (CDDL) Version 1.1, commercial support is available for those that need it.

In this book, we will focus on Payara Micro, with an emphasis on Payara's implementation of MicroProfile APIs.

# CHAPTER 2

# Developing Microservices Using Payara Micro

Microservices are nothing but RESTful web services; they typically perform a single task; as such, their code bases tend to be small. In a microservices architecture, applications are composed of several different microservices communicating with one another.

Payara Micro is a MicroProfile-compliant runtime; as such, applications deployed with Payara Micro must conform to the MicroProfile specification. MicroProfile uses the Jakarta RESTful Web Services API for RESTful web services deployment. In this chapter, we will see how to develop RESTful web services using said API and execute them against Payara Micro.

## Setting Up Your Environment

Payara provides a Maven plug-in that makes working with Payara Micro projects easier. In this section, we will discuss how to set up Maven projects for Payara Micro applications.

---

NetBeans IDE can create a Payara Micro project out of the box with all necessary configuration in place.

---

## Payara Micro Maven Plug-in

To add the Payara Micro Maven plug-in to your project, add it to the `<plugins>` section of your *pom.xml* as illustrated in the following example.

© David R. Heffelfinger 2022
D. R. Heffelfinger, *Payara Micro Revealed*, https://doi.org/10.1007/978-1-4842-8161-1_2

```
<build>
  <plugins>
    <plugin>
      <groupId>fish.payara.maven.plugins</groupId>
      <artifactId>payara-micro-maven-plugin</artifactId>
      <version>1.4.0</version>
      <configuration>
        <payaraVersion>5.2021.5</payaraVersion>
        <deployWar>false</deployWar>
        <commandLineOptions>
          <option>
            <key>--autoBindHttp</key>
          </option>
          <option>
            <key>--deploy</key>
            <value>
             ${project.build.directory}/${project.build.finalName}
            </value>
          </option>
        </commandLineOptions>
        <contextRoot>/</contextRoot>
      </configuration>
    </plugin>
  </plugins>
</build>
```

Under the `<configuration>` section, we can set several configuration options used when running our application in Payara Micro.

Maven automatically downloads the Payara Micro version we specify in the `<payaraVersion>` tag.

We can specify if we want to automatically deploy the project WAR file in the `<deployWar>` tag. Usually when developing an application, it makes sense to deploy the application as an exploded WAR file (more on that later); therefore, it is a good idea to set this value to `false`.

We can specify command-line options to pass to Payara Micro in the `<commandLineOptions>` tag. Table 2-1 lists the options that are available.

***Table 2-1.*** *Payara Micro Command-Line Options*

| Command-Line Option | Description |
|---|---|
| autoBindHttp | If set to true, Payara Micro will automatically find an available port and bind it as the HTTP port |
| deploy | Specifies either an exploded or standard WAR file to Payara Micro. As illustrated in the example, it is a good idea to take advantage of Maven environment variables when deploying our project from Maven |
| port | If autoBindHttp is set to false, used to specify the HTTP port to use |

The complete list of command-line options for Payara Micro can be found at *https://docs.payara.fish/community/docs/documentation/payara-micro/appendices/cmd-line-opts.html*.

Additionally, we can specify the context root of our application via the <contextRoot> tag. In a microservices application, there is typically only one RESTful web service per application; therefore, typically, we would use the root context ("/") here.

# Payara BOM

Maven Bill of Materials (BOM) are a special kind of POM used to keep dependencies in sync. Payara provides a BOM that provides all necessary dependencies for Payara Micro. In order to successfully build and deploy our code to Payara Micro, we need to include the Payara BOM in the <dependencyManagement> section of our *pom.xml* file. For example:

```
<dependencyManagement>
  <dependencies>
    <dependency>
      <groupId>fish.payara.api</groupId>
      <artifactId>payara-bom</artifactId>
      <version>${version.payara}</version>
```

```
    <type>pom</type>
    <scope>import</scope>
  </dependency>
  </dependencies>
</dependencyManagement>
```

## Payara Maven Repository

In order to find Payara-specific dependencies, we need to add the Payara Maven Repository to the `<repositories>` section of our *pom.xml*.

```
<repositories>
 <repository>
   <id>payara-nexus-artifacts</id>
   <name>Payara Nexus Artifacts</name>
   <url>https://nexus.payara.fish/repository/payara-artifacts</url>
   <releases>
     <enabled>true</enabled>
   </releases>
   <snapshots>
     <enabled>false</enabled>
   </snapshots>
 </repository>
</repositories>
```

Nexus is a popular open source repository management tool. The Payara Maven Repository uses Nexus to manage its Maven artifacts.

## Jakarta EE and MicroProfile Dependencies

Last but not least, we need to add dependencies for any Jakarta EE or MicroProfile APIs we will use in our project. Our simple example uses only the Jakarta RESTful Web Services API; therefore, we only need one dependency.

```
<dependencies>
  <dependency>
    <groupId>jakarta.platform</groupId>
    <artifactId>jakarta.jakartaee-web-api</artifactId>
    <scope>provided</scope>
  </dependency>
</dependencies>
```

# Specifying the Base URI for Our Web Services

Before we can start developing RESTful web services, we need to specify the base URI that all web service endpoints in our module will share. This can be done via the @ApplicationConfig annotation, as illustrated in the following example.

```
package com.ensode.microservice;

import javax.ws.rs.ApplicationPath;
import javax.ws.rs.core.Application;

@ApplicationPath("webresources")
public class ApplicationConfig extends Application {

}
```

The annotated class must extend the Application class; the value of the ApplicationPath annotation corresponds to the root URI of our RESTful web services (webresources, in our example). The root URI we specify here will precede the URIs of the RESTful web services we develop; for example, if we write a RESTful web service with a "sample" URI, the complete URI for the web service would be /webresources/sample.

# Running Our Application

Maven can create an exploded WAR file from any Java web project via the war:exploded goal. Similarly, we can start Payara Micro straight from Maven via the payara-micro:start Maven goal provided by the Payara Micro Maven Project.

By invoking Maven using the aforementioned two Maven goals, we can start Payara Micro and automatically deploy our application code.

```
mvn war:exploded payara-micro:start
```

11

We should see some output in the command line similar to the following:

```
[2021-08-07T13:21:06.418-0400] [] [INFO] [] [PayaraMicro] [tid: _ThreadID=1
_ThreadName=main] [timeMillis: 1628356866418] [levelValue: 800] [[

Payara Micro URLs:
http://192.168.1.165:8080/

'microservice-1.0-SNAPSHOT' REST Endpoints:
GET      /openapi/
GET      /openapi/application.wadl
GET      /webresources/application.wadl
DELETE   /webresources/sample
GET      /webresources/sample
PATCH    /webresources/sample
POST     /webresources/sample
PUT      /webresources/sample

]]

[2021-08-07T13:21:06.418-0400] [] [INFO] [] [PayaraMicro] [tid: _ThreadID=1
_ThreadName=main] [timeMillis: 1628356866418] [levelValue: 800] Payara
Micro  5.2021.4 #badassmicrofish (build 740) ready in 7,751 (ms)
Handling HTTP GET requests
```

Notice that the output specifies the IP address and HTTP port where Payara Micro is listening, as well as all RESTful web service endpoints along with the HTTP request types they listen for.

---

Some of these endpoints are automatically generated by Payara Micro.

---

Starting our application this way, combined with the compile-on-save feature most modern Java IDEs possess, allows us to hot deploy our application, meaning that code changes are automatically picked up by Payara Micro as we save our code, eliminating the need to manually build and run our code to test our code changes.

# Developing RESTful Web Services

In order to turn any plain old Java object into a RESTful web service, all we need to do is annotate it with the @Path annotation. This annotation allows us to specify the URI for our web service; it also lets the runtime (Payara Micro, in our case) know that this class is a web service.

```
package com.ensode.microservice;

@Path("sample")
public class SampleRestFulService {
}
```

The @Path annotation, combined with the @ApplicationPath annotation we previously discussed, determines the full URI of our RESTful web service. In our sample project, the complete URI for the RESTful web service would be webresources/sample.

A RESTful web service needs to respond to one or more HTTP request types (GET, POST, PUT, DELETE, or PATCH); this is accomplished via method-level annotations.

# Handling HTTP GET Requests

We can handle HTTP GET requests in our RESTful web services by annotating one of our methods with the @GET annotation. If our method returns a value to the client, we need to specify the mime type of the returned value via the @Produces annotation.

```
@GET
@Produces(MediaType.APPLICATION_JSON)
public String processGetRequest() {

  String json = "{"
    + "\"msg\":\"Service processed HTTP GET request!\""
    + "}";

  return json;
}
```

JSON is by far the most common mime type used for data transmission in RESTful web services and microservices, but it is by no means the only one. All supported mime types are defined as constants in the MediaType class; others supported include XML (MediaType.TEXT_XML), HTML (MediaType.TEXT_HTML), and plain text (MediaType. TEXT_PLAIN), among others.

---

Use your IDE Code Completion on the MediaType class to see all supported mime types.

---

In our simple example, we are simply hard-coding a JSON string and returning that. Typically, we would process some data and generate a JSON string with one of Jakarta EE's JSON processing libraries (JSON-B or JSON-P). We will cover JSON processing later in the book.

# Handling HTTP POST Requests

HTTP POST requests are handled via the @POST annotation; usage is identical to the previously discussed @GET annotation.

```
@POST
@Produces(MediaType.APPLICATION_JSON)
public String processPostRequest() {

    String json = "{"
            + "\"msg\":\"Service processed HTTP POST request!\""
            + "}";

    return json;
}
```

This example is nearly identical to the one in the previous section, the main difference being we annotated our method with the @POST annotation, which causes the method to be invoked when our service responds to an HTTP POST request.

# Handling HTTP PUT Requests

HTTP PUT requests are handled via the @PUT annotation.

```
@PUT
@Produces(MediaType.APPLICATION_JSON)
public String processPutRequest() {

  String json = "{"
          + "\"msg\":\"Service processed HTTP PUT request!\""
          + "}";

  return json;
}
```

The @PUT annotation on this method causes the method to be invoked when our service responds to an HTTP PUT request.

# Handling HTTP DELETE Requests

HTTP DELETE requests are handled via the @DELETE annotation.

```
@DELETE
@Produces(MediaType.APPLICATION_JSON)
public String processDeleteRequest() {

  String json = "{"
          + "\"msg\":\"Service processed HTTP DELETE request!\""
          + "}";

  return json;
}
```

The @DELETE annotation on this method causes the method to be invoked when our service responds to an HTTP DELETE request.

## Handling HTTP PATCH Requests

We can also handle HTTP PATCH requests via the @PATCH annotation.

```
@PATCH
@Produces(MediaType.APPLICATION_JSON)
public String processPatchRequest() {

  String json = "{"
          + "\"msg\":\"Service processed HTTP PATCH request!\""
          + "}";

  return json;
}
```

As expected, the @PATCH annotation on this method causes the method to be invoked when our service responds to an HTTP PATCH request.

# Path and Query Parameters

You can pass parameters to a RESTful web service; there are two ways to do that: using path parameters and query parameters; both ways are supported by the Jakarta RESTful Web Services API.

## Path Parameters

Path parameters are added to a RESTful web services path when invoked; for example, the following RESTful web service URI contains two path parameters; the first parameter value is "Mr"; the second one is "Heffelfinger".

*http://localhost:8080/webresources/pathparams/Mr/Heffelfinger*

In order for our RESTful web services to accept path parameters, we need to add the @Path annotation at the method level, as well as the @PathParam annotation for each method argument corresponding to a path parameter.

```java
package com.ensode.pathparams;

//imports omitted

@Path("pathparams")
public class PathParamsSampleService {

  @GET
  @Produces(MediaType.APPLICATION_JSON)
  @Path("/{title}/{lastName}")
  public String sayFormalHello(@PathParam("title") String title,
      @PathParam("lastName") String lastName) {
    return String.format("{\n"
            + "  \"msg\":\"Hello, %s %s\"\n"
            + "}", title, lastName);
  }

}
```

The method-level @Path annotation provides a URI template, specifying the location of each path parameter. In our example, the first parameter is called title; the second parameter is called lastName; we specify the order in which we expect path parameters by using the @Path annotation in this manner.

To bind path parameters to method arguments, we used the @PathParameter annotation as illustrated in the example; notice that the value of the @PathParameter annotation must match the name of the URI template variables specified in the method-level @Path annotation (title and lastName, in our example).

When a client invokes our service, it is expected for the client to pass the expected parameters in the right order; for example, we could invoke our service using curl as follows:

```
curl http://localhost:8080/webresources/pathparams/Mr/Heffelfinger
```

In this case, *Mr* corresponds to the value of our first parameter, as defined in the URI template of the method-level *@Path* annotation; *Heffelfinger* corresponds to the second path parameter, again defined in the URI template; these values are automatically bound to the corresponding method arguments by annotating these arguments with the *@PathParam* annotation whose values match the URI variables defined in the URI template (*title* and *lastName*, in our example).

Once we invoke our service, it will return a JSON string with the corresponding values.

```
{
  "msg":"Hello, Mr Heffelfinger"
}
```

# Query Parameters

The second way we can pass parameters to our RESTful web services is via query parameters. In this case, parameters are sent as a query containing name value pairs in the URI for our web service.

For example, using curl, we could pass query parameters to a RESTful web service endpoint as follows:

```
curl "http://localhost:8080/webresources/queryparams?title=Mr&lastName=
Heffelfinger"
```

In this example, the URI for the RESTful web service endpoint is `http://localhost:8080/webresources/queryparams`; this example has two parameters, named `title` and `lastName`. A question mark is used to delimit the boundary between the URI and the query.

```
package com.ensode.queryparams;

//imports omitted

@Path("queryparams")
public class QueryParamsSampleService {

  @GET
  @Produces(MediaType.APPLICATION_JSON)
  public String sayFormalHello(@QueryParam("title") String title,
    @QueryParam("lastName") String lastName) {
    return String.format("{\n"
            + "  \"msg\":\"Hello, %s %s\"\n"
            + "}", title, lastName);
  }

}
```

Parameter names are defined by the @QueryParam annotation; values sent by the client are automatically bound to the corresponding method arguments. Output of this example would be identical to the path parameters examples we discussed in the previous section.

# Parsing JSON Data

RESTful web services can consume and produce data in various formats, with JSON being by far the most common one.

Jakarta RESTful Web Services can automatically convert JSON data to and from Java with almost no effort on our part. Having a Java class with fields matching a JSON string's properties will result in those fields being automatically populated with the corresponding values. All we need to do is annotate our method with the @Consumes and @Produces annotations using the appropriate media type.

```
package com.ensode.jsonprocessing;

//imports omitted

@Path("messageprocessor")
public class MessageProcessor {

  @PUT
  @Consumes(MediaType.APPLICATION_JSON)
  @Produces(MediaType.APPLICATION_JSON)
  public Message processMessage(Message message) {
    Message returnedMessage = new Message();

    returnedMessage.setMsgText(message.getMsgText().
      toUpperCase());

    return returnedMessage;
  }
}
```

Our Message class is a simple POJO (plain old Java object).

```
package com.ensode.jsonprocessing;

public class Message {

  private String msgText;

  public String getMsgText() {
    return msgText;
  }

  public void setMsgText(String msgText) {
    this.msgText = msgText;
  }

}
```

In our example, the client is expected to send a JSON string that can be parsed into a Message object. By simply annotating our method with the @Consumes annotation and specifying *application/JSON* as the media type, data from the client is used to automatically populate an instance of our Message class.

We could invoke our service using curl as follows:

```
curl -X PUT http://localhost:8080/webresources/messageprocessor -H
"Content-Type: application/json" -d '{"msgText":"Yay for seamless JSON
parsing!"}'
```

Notice that the JSON data we are sending to the service has a msgText property; this property is used to populate the corresponding msgText instance variable in our Message class.

Our example service method returns another instance of the Message class, since we are using the @Produces annotation with a media type of *application/json*; this return value is automatically converted to a JSON string, which we can see in the output of the preceding curl command.

```
{"msgText":"YAY FOR SEAMLESS JSON PARSING!"}
```

# Summary

In this chapter, we saw how we can develop RESTful web services with the Jakarta RESTful Web Services API. We saw how using a few simple annotations can convert a Java class to a RESTful web service and handle HTTP requests, including GET, PUT, POST, DELETE, and PATCH requests.

We also covered parameters to our RESTful web services. We saw how to process path parameters via the `@PathParam` annotation. Additionally, we saw how to process query parameters via the `@QueryParam` annotation.

Finally, we saw how we can seamlessly parse JSON strings and populate our Java objects and how to easily generate JSON strings from plain old Java objects.

# CHAPTER 3

# Developing Microservice Clients

In a typical microservice architecture, an application is composed from a number of independently developed and deployed microservices. These microservices need to communicate with one another over the network. By far, the most common way to implement this functionality is to have microservices developed as RESTful web services, with some microservices acting as RESTful web service clients for others.

Payara Micro supports the MicroProfile REST client API, which greatly simplifies the development of RESTful web service clients.

## MicroProfile REST Client API Overview

The MicroProfile REST client API makes developing RESTful web service clients very easy, especially if we are developing clients for RESTful web services developed with Jakarta RESTful Web Services (covered in Chapter 2).

Essentially, a MicroProfile RESTful web service client consists of a sole Java interface with method signatures matching the corresponding RESTful web service method signature (i.e., same method name and parameters).

At the class level, a MicroProfile REST client interface uses the @Path annotation; its value argument must match the corresponding @Path annotation on the service.

Each abstract method on a MicroProfile REST client interface must have the same annotations as the corresponding method on the server (@Path, @PUT, @Consumes, @Produces, etc.).

© David R. Heffelfinger 2022
D. R. Heffelfinger, *Payara Micro Revealed*, https://doi.org/10.1007/978-1-4842-8161-1_3

In practice, the easiest way to develop a MicroProfile REST client is to copy the source code for the service, change the class to an interface, and remove all method bodies. At this point, we are 95% done with "developing" our RESTful web client.

Once we have an interface matching our service, we need to add the @RegisterRestClient annotation at the interface level; this annotation indicates that the interface is a RESTful web service client.

A typical RESTful web service client interface looks like the following:

```
package com.ensode.jsonparsingclient;
//Imports omitted

@RegisterRestClient
@Path("messageprocessor")
public interface MessageProcessorClient {

    @PUT
    @Consumes(MediaType.APPLICATION_JSON)
    @Produces(MediaType.APPLICATION_JSON)
    public Message processMessage(Message message);
}
```

This example is a RESTful web service client for the service we developed in the "Parsing JSON Data" section in the previous chapter. Notice that all annotations match their counterparts on the source code for the service.

Please note that we don't (and shouldn't) write an implementation for our RESTful web service client interfaces; the implementation is generated at runtime by Payara Micro (or any MicroProfile-compliant runtime). If we don't write an implementation for our RESTful web service client, then how do we specify the URI of the service we are interacting with? The answer lies in the MicroProfile Config API.

We will cover the MicroProfile API in detail later in the book; for now, we will just cover what is necessary to indicate the URI of the service we are interacting with.

In order to specify the URI of our service, we need to create a file called *microprofile-config.properties* and place it in a directory called META-INF in the root of our WAR file. If using Maven, this file must be placed under *src/resources/META-INF*; Maven will place it in the right location in our WAR file when we build.

We need a single property per RESTful web service client in our application; the property name must follow the following format:

*<fully qualified RESTful client interface name>/mp-rest/url*

In our example, the property name would be

*com.ensode.jsonparsingclient.MessageProcessorClient/mp-rest/url*

The value of the property must match the URI for our service, including the root URL defined in the Application class; in our example, the URI for our service is

*http://localhost:8080/webresources*

Therefore, the name/value pair in our microprofile-config property file would look as follows:

```
com.ensode.jsonparsingclient.MessageProcessorClient/mp-rest/url=http://
localhost:8080/webresources
```

This section described the general pattern we need to follow to develop RESTful web service clients using the MicroProfile REST client API. Next, we will cover specifics for each type of HTTP requests, path and query parameters, and passing data to the services in the body of our requests.

To use our REST client interface, we need to inject it into another artifact (typically a RESTful web service developed against the Jakarta RESTful Web Services API) via CDI's @Inject annotation, plus the @RestClient annotation provided by the MicroProfile REST client API.

```
@ApplicationScoped
public class MessageProcessorRestClient {

  private static final Logger LOGGER = Logger.getLogger(MessageProcessor
  RestClient.class.getName());

  @Inject
  @RestClient
  private MessageProcessorClient messageProcessorClient;
```

```
public void init(@Observes @Initialized(ApplicationScoped.class)
  Object object) {

  Message message = new Message();
  Message returnedMessage;

  message.setMsgText(
    "Hello from the MicroProfile REST client!");

  returnedMessage =
    messageProcessorClient.processMessage(message);

  LOGGER.log(Level.INFO, String.format(
    "Server returned the following message: %s",
    returnedMessage.getMsgText()));
  }
}
```

In this example, we are using a Jakarta Contexts and Dependency Injection (CDI) trick to execute code upon application initialization.

Notice the @Observes @Initialized(ApplicationScoped.class) annotations on the object parameter of the init() method; these annotations cause the init() method to be executed by the runtime when the CDI application scope is initialized, which happens to coincide to when the application has been fully deployed. This trick allows us to run any arbitrary Java code when our application is initialized, combined with the ability to launch MicroProfile applications from the command line; this trick allows us to write simple command-line test clients for our RESTful web services.

---

CDI is covered in detail later in the book.

---

We just described the general pattern to develop REST client applications using the MicroProfile REST client API; in the following sections, we'll go into some specifics.

# Generating HTTP GET Requests

To handle HTTP GET requests, our REST client interface needs to be annotated with the @Path and @RegisterRestClient annotations; the value of the @Path annotation needs to match the value of the service we are calling. HTTP GET requests are handled by the

@GET annotation; if the RESTful web service method we are calling returns a response, it will typically be a JSON string; therefore, we should add the @Produces annotation with the appropriate value; matching the annotations and values of the service we are calling will typically yield the desired results.

The following code snippet illustrates a typical RESTful web service client interface that sends an HTTP GET request to a RESTful web service:

```
@Path("sample")
@RegisterRestClient
public interface SampleRestfulServiceClient {

  @GET
  @Produces(value = MediaType.APPLICATION_JSON)
  String processGetRequest();

}
```

We specify the URI of the RESTful web service we are calling via the *microprofile-config.properties* file.

```
com.ensode.restclient.SampleRestfulServiceClient/mp-rest/url=http://
localhost:8080/webresources
```

Recall that the root URI must match the value defined in the Application class in the RESTful web service project.

We can then inject our interface via CDI in order to invoke the method and generate the GET request. We inject the interface via the @Inject and @RestClient annotations. An implementation of our interface is automatically generated and injected; we then simply invoke the method annotated with @GET to generate the GET request and optionally store the response in a variable.

The following example illustrates this process:

```
package com.ensode.restclient;

//imports omitted

@ApplicationScoped
public class RestfulClient {

  private static final Logger LOGGER =
    Logger.getLogger(RestfulClient.class.getName());
```

```
@Inject
@RestClient
private SampleRestfulServiceClient sampleRestfulServiceClient;

public void init(
  @Observes @Initialized(ApplicationScoped.class)
  Object object) {
  String returnedGetData;

  LOGGER.log(Level.INFO, "--- Sending HTTP GET request ");
  returnedGetData =
    sampleRestfulServiceClient.processGetRequest();

  LOGGER.log(Level.INFO, String.format(
    "--- GET request response: %s", returnedGetData));
  }
}
```

We can run our client application in Payara Micro by invoking the `war:exploded` and `payara-micro:start` Maven goals from the command line.

```
mvn war:exploded payara-micro:start
```

We should see the expected output of our log statement on the Payara Micro output on the console:

```
[2021-08-20T14:58:59.463-0400] [] [INFO] [] [com.ensode.restclient.
RestfulClient] [tid: _ThreadID=1 _ThreadName=main] [timeMillis:
1629485939463] [levelValue: 800] --- GET request response: {"msg":"Service
processed HTTP GET request!"}
```

which is the expected output from the service we are invoking, which we developed in Chapter 2.

## Generating HTTP POST Requests

To handle HTTP POST requests, our REST client interface needs to be annotated with the @Path and @RegisterRestClient annotations as usual; the value of the @Path annotation once again needs to match the value of the service we are calling. HTTP POST requests are handled by the @POST annotation; if the RESTful web service method we are calling returns a response, it will typically be a JSON string; therefore, we should add the @Produces annotation with the appropriate value.

The following code snippet illustrates a typical RESTful web service client interface that sends an HTTP POST request to a RESTful web service:

```
@Path("sample")
@RegisterRestClient
public interface SampleRestfulServiceClient {

  @POST
  @Produces(value = MediaType.APPLICATION_JSON)
  String processPostRequest();

}
```

As is the case for other HTTP request types, we specify the URI of the RESTful web service we are calling via the *microprofile-config.properties* file.

```
com.ensode.restclient.SampleRestfulServiceClient/mp-rest/url=http://
localhost:8080/webresources
```

We need to make sure the root URI of the service matches the value defined in the Application class in the RESTful web service project.

We then use the CDI @Inject and @RestClient annotations to annotate the interface. Finally, we simply invoke the method annotated with @POST to generate the POST request and optionally store the response in a variable.

```
package com.ensode.restclient;

//imports omitted

@ApplicationScoped
public class RestfulClient {

  private static final Logger LOGGER =
    Logger.getLogger(RestfulClient.class.getName());

  @Inject
  @RestClient
  private SampleRestfulServiceClient sampleRestfulServiceClient;
```

```
public void init(
  @Observes @Initialized(ApplicationScoped.class)
  Object object) {
  String returnedPostData;

  LOGGER.log(Level.INFO, "--- Sending HTTP POST request ");
  returnedPostData =
    sampleRestfulServiceClient.processPostRequest();

  LOGGER.log(Level.INFO, String.format(
    "--- POST request response: %s", returnedPostData));
  }
}
```

When we run our client application via the usual Maven goals, we should see the expected output from the service.

```
[2021-08-20T14:58:59.463-0400] [] [INFO] [] [com.ensode.restclient.
RestfulClient] [tid: _ThreadID=1 _ThreadName=main] [timeMillis:
1629485939463] [levelValue: 800] --- POST request response: {"msg":"Service
processed HTTP POST request!"}
```

# Generating HTTP PUT Requests

For HTTP PUT requests, our REST client interface needs to be annotated with the @Path and @RegisterRestClient annotations as is the case for other HTTP request types; the value of the @Path annotation, unsurprisingly, needs to match the value of the service we are calling. HTTP PUT requests are handled by the @PUT annotation; if the RESTful web service method we are calling returns a response, it will typically be a JSON string; therefore, we should add the @Produces annotation as usual, with the appropriate value.

The following code snippet illustrates a typical RESTful web service client interface that sends an HTTP PUT request to a RESTful web service:

```
@Path("sample")
@RegisterRestClient
public interface SampleRestfulServiceClient {

  @PUT
```

```
@Produces(value = MediaType.APPLICATION_JSON)
String processPutRequest();
```

}

As usual, we specify the URI of the RESTful web service we are calling via the *microprofile-config.properties* file.

```
com.ensode.restclient.SampleRestfulServiceClient/mp-rest/url=http://
localhost:8080/webresources
```

We need to make sure the root URI of the service matches the value defined in the Application class in the RESTful web service project.

We then inject our interface via the CDI @Inject and @RestClient annotations as usual; then we simply invoke the method annotated with @PUT to generate the PUT request and optionally store the response in a variable.

```
package com.ensode.restclient;

//imports omitted

@ApplicationScoped
public class RestfulClient {

  private static final Logger LOGGER =
    Logger.getLogger(RestfulClient.class.getName());

  @Inject
  @RestClient
  private SampleRestfulServiceClient sampleRestfulServiceClient;

  public void init(
    @Observes @Initialized(ApplicationScoped.class)
    Object object) {
    String returnedPutData;

    LOGGER.log(Level.INFO, "--- Sending HTTP PUT request ");
    returnedPutData =
      sampleRestfulServiceClient.processPutRequest();
```

```
    LOGGER.log(Level.INFO, String.format(
      "--- PUT request response: %s", returnedPutData));
  }
}
```

After running our client application in Payara Micro, we can see the body of the response sent by the service in Payara Micro's command-line output.

[2021-08-20T14:58:59.463-0400] [] [INFO] [] [com.ensode.restclient.
RestfulClient] [tid: _ThreadID=1 _ThreadName=main] [timeMillis:
1629485939463] [levelValue: 800] **--- PUT request response: {"msg":"Service
processed HTTP PUT request!"}**

# Generating HTTP DELETE Requests

When generating HTTP DELETE requests, our REST client interface, unsurprisingly, needs to be annotated with the @Path and @RegisterRestClient annotations; the value of the @Path annotation needs to match the value of the corresponding annotation on the service we are calling. HTTP DELETE requests are handled by the @DELETE annotation; if the RESTful web service method we are calling returns a response, it will typically be a JSON string; therefore, we should add the @Produces annotation as usual, with the appropriate value.

The following code snippet illustrates a typical RESTful web service client interface that sends an HTTP DELETE request to a RESTful web service:

```
@Path("sample")
@RegisterRestClient
public interface SampleRestfulServiceClient {

  @DELETE
  @Produces(value = MediaType.APPLICATION_JSON)
  String processDeleteRequest();

}
```

Again, we specify the URI of the RESTful web service we are calling via the *microprofile-config.properties* file.

```
com.ensode.restclient.SampleRestfulServiceClient/mp-rest/url=http://
localhost:8080/webresources
```

As is the case for other HTTP request types, we need to make sure the root URI of the service matches the value defined in the `Application` class in the RESTful web service project.

To generate the DELETE request, we need to inject our interface via the CDI `@Inject` and `@RestClient` annotations; then we invoke the method annotated with `@DELETE` and optionally store the response in a variable.

```
package com.ensode.restclient;

//imports omitted

@ApplicationScoped
public class RestfulClient {

  private static final Logger LOGGER =
    Logger.getLogger(RestfulClient.class.getName());

  @Inject
  @RestClient
  private SampleRestfulServiceClient sampleRestfulServiceClient;

  public void init(
    @Observes @Initialized(ApplicationScoped.class)
    Object object) {
    String returnedDeleteData;

    LOGGER.log(Level.INFO, "--- Sending HTTP DELETE request ");
    returnedDeleteData =
      sampleRestfulServiceClient.processDeleteRequest();

    LOGGER.log(Level.INFO, String.format(
      "--- DELETE request response: %s", returnedDeleteData));
  }
}
```

After we run our application, we should be able to see the server response in Payara Micro's command-line output.

```
[2021-08-20T14:58:59.463-0400] [] [INFO] [] [com.ensode.restclient.
RestfulClient] [tid: _ThreadID=1 _ThreadName=main] [timeMillis:
1629485939463] [levelValue: 800] --- DELETE request response:
{"msg":"Service processed HTTP DELETE request!"}
```

# Path and Query Parameters

Just like we can develop our RESTful web services to accept path and query parameters, we can develop clients to pass them; all we need to do is annotate our methods on the REST client interface with the same annotations used on the service.

## Path Parameters

To pass path parameters to a RESTful web service, we use the @Path annotation, providing a URI template designating the position of each parameter; additionally, we need to annotate each method argument with the @PathParam annotation; the value of this annotation must match the corresponding parameter in the URI template defined in the @Path annotation for our method.

```
package com.ensode.pathparamsclient;

//imports omitted

@RegisterRestClient
@Path("pathparams")
public interface PathParamsSampleServiceClient {

    @GET
    @Produces(MediaType.APPLICATION_JSON)
    @Path("/{title}/{lastName}")
    public String sayFormalHello(@PathParam("title") String title,
    @PathParam("lastName") String lastName);

}
```

If all of this looks familiar, it's because the exact same annotations are used on the RESTful web service to define path parameters accepted by the service. This consistency makes it very easy to develop clients against services developed using the Jakarta RESTful Web Services API.

We then can inject our RESTful interface using the @RestClient and @Inject annotations as usual. To pass our path parameters to the service, we simply invoke the appropriate method in our RESTful client interface with appropriate arguments.

```
package com.ensode.pathparamsclient;

//imports omitted

@ApplicationScoped
public class PathParamRestfulClient {

  @Inject
  @RestClient
  private PathParamsSampleServiceClient
    pathParamsSampleServiceClient;
  private static final Logger LOGGER =
    Logger.getLogger(PathParamRestfulClient.class.getName());

  public void init(@Observes @Initialized(ApplicationScoped.class)
    Object object) {
    String formalResponse;

    formalResponse =
      pathParamsSampleServiceClient.sayFormalHello("Mr",
      "Heffelfinger");

    LOGGER.log(Level.INFO, String.format(
      "Received the following formal response: %s",
      formalResponse));
  }
}
```

After running our application in Payara Micro, we can see the response from the service in its command-line output.

```
[2021-08-20T15:06:24.930-0400] [] [INFO] [] [com.ensode.pathparamsclient.
PathParamRestfulClient] [tid: _ThreadID=1 _ThreadName=main] [timeMillis:
1629486384930] [levelValue: 800] [[
  Received the following formal response: {
  "msg":"Hello, Mr Heffelfinger"
}]]
```

# Query Parameters

If we need to pass query parameters to a RESTful web service, we can do so by
annotating our method arguments with the @QueryParam annotation. This annotation
indicates the query parameter name each method argument will populate.

```
package com.ensode.queryparamsclient;

//imports omitted

@RegisterRestClient
@Path("queryparams")
public interface QueryParamsSampleServiceClient {

  @GET
  @Produces(MediaType.APPLICATION_JSON)
  public String sayFormalHello(@QueryParam("title") String title,
    @QueryParam("lastName") String lastName);

}
```

Unsurprisingly, the process to create a client that generates query parameters is
pretty much identical to the process of creating a server that accepts them.

To pass the query parameters, we inject our client interface via the @RestClient
and @Inject annotations as usual and then call its corresponding method with the
appropriate arguments.

```
package com.ensode.queryparamsclient;

//imports omitted

@ApplicationScoped
public class QueryParamsRestfulClient {
```

```
private static final Logger LOGGER =
  Logger.getLogger(QueryParamsRestfulClient.class.getName());

@Inject
@RestClient
private QueryParamsSampleServiceClient
 queryParamsSampleServiceClient;

public void init(@Observes @Initialized(ApplicationScoped.class)
  Object object) {

  String serverResponse;

  serverResponse =
    queryParamsSampleServiceClient.sayFormalHello("Mr",
    "Heffelfinger");

  LOGGER.log(Level.INFO, String.format(
    "Received the following response: %s", serverResponse));
  }
}
```

When running our client application in Payara Micro, we can see the response sent by the service.

```
[2021-08-20T15:08:51.480-0400] [] [INFO] [] [com.ensode.queryparamsclient.
QueryParamsRestfulClient] [tid: _ThreadID=1 _ThreadName=main] [timeMillis:
1629486531480] [levelValue: 800] [[
  Received the following response: {
  "msg":"Hello, Mr Heffelfinger"
}]]
```

# Generating JSON from Java Objects

Any JSON string we need to pass to the service we are invoking needs to be added as a parameter to the method we are invoking. The assumption is that the service will accept a JSON string as the body of the request adhering to the structure of our Java class.

```
package com.ensode.jsonparsingclient;

//imports omitted

@RegisterRestClient
@Path("messageprocessor")
public interface MessageProcessorClient {

  @PUT
  @Consumes(MediaType.APPLICATION_JSON)
  @Produces(MediaType.APPLICATION_JSON)
  public Message processMessage(Message message);
}
```

The MicroProfile REST client API automates the conversion from Java objects to JSON. If we have a Java class with the same structure as the JSON we need to generate, we can simply instantiate the class as usual and pass it as a parameter to the REST client interface method generating the HTTP request.

For example, if we needed to generate a JSON string like the following:

```
{
  "msgText":"Hello from the MicroProfile REST client!"
}
```

we could simply create a Java class with a `String` property matching the key name in our JSON string.

```
package com.ensode.jsonparsingclient;

public class Message {

  private String msgText;

  //getter and setter omitted
}
```

We then simply instantiate our class, populate its property, and pass it as a parameter to the appropriate method; serialization into a JSON string is done for us automatically.

```java
package com.ensode.jsonparsingclient;

//imports omitted

@ApplicationScoped
public class MessageProcessorRestClient {

  private static final Logger LOGGER = Logger.getLogger(MessageProcessor
  RestClient.class.getName());

  @Inject
  @RestClient
  private MessageProcessorClient messageProcessorClient;

  public void init(@Observes @Initialized(ApplicationScoped.class) Object
  object) {

    Message message = new Message();
    Message returnedMessage;

    message.setMsgText(
      "Hello from the MicroProfile REST client!");

    returnedMessage =
      messageProcessorClient.processMessage(message);

    LOGGER.log(Level.INFO, String.format("Server returned the following
    message: %s", returnedMessage.getMsgText()));
  }
}
```

As we can see, all JSON processing is handled automatically for us by the
MicroProfile REST client API. As a matter of fact, if we are developing both the service
and the client, there is no need to handle JSON directly at all, as the Jakarta RESTful Web
Services API handles the conversion on the service and, as we just saw, the MicroProfile
REST client API handles the conversion on the client.

---

If, for any reason, we need to handle raw JSON, we can simply use String as the
parameter type on our method signatures.

---

# Summary

In this chapter, we saw how we can create RESTful web service clients using the MicroProfile REST client API. We covered how we can create a client by writing a Java interface with a few simple annotations, without even having to create an implementation for the interface. We also discussed how to send different types of HTTP requests, including GET, PUT, POST, and DELETE. We saw how creating RESTful clients for services created with the Jakarta RESTful Web Service API is so simple it's almost trivial, as all method signatures and annotations follow the pattern established in the client.

Additionally, we covered how to pass parameters to RESTful web services that require them, including both path and query parameters.

Finally, we covered how to add a JSON body to our HTTP requests and how the MicroProfile REST client API takes care of most of the grunt work of JSON handling for us.

# CHAPTER 4

# Contexts and Dependency Injection

Contexts and Dependency Injection (CDI) is a powerful dependency injection mechanism that is part of both the Jakarta EE and MicroProfile specifications. CDI allows us to easily inject dependencies into our code; it also has an event handling mechanism that allows us to loosely couple different parts of our code. In this chapter, we will see how we can incorporate CDI into our MicroProfile applications deployed to Payara Micro.

## CDI Scopes

CDI beans have *scopes*, which denote their life cycle; a bean's scope indicates when the bean is created and destroyed. CDI beans are given a scope by annotating them with one of the scope annotations; for example, to configure a CDI bean to have a request scope, it needs to be annotated with the @RequestScoped annotation.

Table 4-1 summarizes all CDI scopes.

© David R. Heffelfinger 2022
D. R. Heffelfinger, *Payara Micro Revealed*, https://doi.org/10.1007/978-1-4842-8161-1_4

***Table 4-1.*** *CDI Scopes*

| Scope | Annotation | Description |
| --- | --- | --- |
| Application | @ApplicationScoped | Initialized during application startup, destroyed when the application shuts down. All users of the application share the same instance of application scoped CDI beans |
| Session | @SessionScoped | Tied to a single HTTP session, each user gets an instance of session scoped CDI beans |
| Request | @RequestScoped | Tied to an HTTP request, bean is created and destroyed for every HTTP request |
| Conversation | @ConversationScoped | Life cycle of a conversation scoped CDI bean spans two or more HTTP requests |
| Dependent | @Dependent | Dependent CDI beans don't have a scope of their own; instead, they are meant to be injected into another CDI bean and inherit their scope. For example, if injected into a request scoped bean, a dependent bean would get a request scope; when injected to a session scoped CDI bean, it would get a session scope and so on |

We can turn almost any Java class into a CDI bean by annotating it with one of the preceding scope annotations. The main requirement for a CDI bean is that the class must not be abstract and most provide a public, no-argument constructor. It is worth pointing out that the session and conversation scopes are better suited for traditional web applications. For a microservices architecture, we typically only use the application, request, and dependent scopes.

# Life Cycle of CDI Beans

CDI scopes define a CDI bean's life cycle, that is, when the bean is created and destroyed. Typically, we don't instantiate CDI beans ourselves; instead, we delegate that job to the runtime (Payara Micro, in our case).

Sometimes, we need to perform some logic right after our bean is initialized, or just before our bean is destroyed; for this purpose, CDI provides the @PostConstruct and @PreDestroy annotations.

Methods annotated with @PostConstruct are invoked by the MicroProfile runtime right after the CDI bean is initialized; conversely, methods annotated with @PreDestroy are automatically invoked just before the bean is destroyed. Methods annotated with either @PostConstruct or @PreDestroy must return void, take no arguments, and must not be static.

We can turn any of our Jakarta EE RESTful Web Services (i.e., classes annotated with @Path) into a CDI bean by adding one of the scope annotations; typically, we would use the @RequestScoped annotation, which results in a new instance of our service being constructed for every request.

---

You could also annotate your RESTful web service with the @ApplicationScoped annotation, which would result in the same instance of the service responding to all requests; this, however, may result in code that scales poorly.

---

The following example illustrates a web service turned into a request scoped CDI bean:

```
package com.ensode.cdiscopes;

//imports omitted

@RequestScoped
@Path("cdiservice")
public class CdiService {

  private static final Logger LOGGER =
    Logger.getLogger(CdiService.class.getName());

  @PostConstruct
  public void init() {
    LOGGER.log(Level.INFO, "init() method called");
  }

  @PreDestroy
  public void cleanup() {
    LOGGER.log(Level.INFO, "cleanup() method called");
  }
```

```
@POST
public void handlePostRequest() {
  LOGGER.log(Level.INFO, "HTTP POST request received");
}

}
```

Notice that we annotated our class with the @RequestScoped annotation; this turns our RESTful web service class into a request scoped CDI bean and grants us all functionality available to CDI beans, such as having callback methods that the runtime can invoke when the bean is initialized or destroyed.

We created two callback methods; we annotated the init() method with the cdi @PostConstruct annotation, which lets the runtime know it needs to call this method right after our class is constructed. Additionally, we annotated the cleanup() method with @PreDestroy; therefore, it will be called automatically just before the bean is destroyed.

---

In our example, we are simply sending some output to the logs in our callback methods. In a typical application, these callback methods are used to perform any necessary initialization, obtain and release resources such as database connections, etc.

---

Since our service is request scoped, a new instance will be created for each HTTP request it handles; therefore, we should see the expected log entries in the Payara Micro output for each HTTP request.

Our application is configured as follows in its Maven pom.xml file:

```
<plugins>
  <plugin>
    <groupId>fish.payara.maven.plugins</groupId>
    <artifactId>payara-micro-maven-plugin</artifactId>
    <version>1.4.0</version>
    <configuration>
      <payaraVersion>${version.payara}</payaraVersion>
      <deployWar>false</deployWar>
      <commandLineOptions>
```

```
    <option>
      <key>--autoBindHttp</key>
    </option>
    <option>
      <key>--deploy</key>
      <value>${project.build.directory}/$
            {project.build.finalName}</value>
    </option>
  </commandLineOptions>
  <contextRoot>/cdiscopes</contextRoot>
</configuration>
</plugin>
</plugins>
```

Notice how we set the context root to /cdiscopes; we therefore need to use this context root when sending an HTTP request to our service.

We run our application on Payara Micro via the usual Maven goals:

```
mvn war:exploded payara-micro:start
```

We can see in the Payara Micro output that our application was deployed successfully and is listening for requests.

```
[2021-08-30T18:21:02.818-0400] [] [INFO] [] [PayaraMicro] [tid: _ThreadID=1
_ThreadName=main] [timeMillis: 1630362062818] [levelValue: 800] [[

Payara Micro URLs:
http://192.168.1.165:8080/cdiscopes

'cdi-scopes-1.0-SNAPSHOT' REST Endpoints:
GET  /cdiscopes/webresources/application.wadl
POST /cdiscopes/webresources/cdiservice

]]

[2021-08-30T18:21:02.818-0400] [] [INFO] [] [PayaraMicro] [tid: _ThreadID=1
_ThreadName=main] [timeMillis: 1630362062818] [levelValue: 800] Payara
Micro  5.2021.6 #badassmicrofish (build 4579) ready in 8,864 (ms)
```

Now we can send a request to our service; since we annotated the method that will handle the request with the @Post annotation, we need to send an HTTP POST request to our service; the easiest way to do this is via the curl command-line utility.

```
curl -X POST http://localhost:8080/cdiscopes/webresources/cdiservice
```

---

As previously discussed, curl is included out of the box with most modern operating systems.

---

We then examine the Payara Micro output.

```
[2021-08-30T18:21:02.818-0400] [] [INFO] [] [PayaraMicro] [tid: _ThreadID=1
_ThreadName=main] [timeMillis: 1630362062818] [levelValue: 800] Payara
Micro  5.2021.6 #badassmicrofish (build 4579) ready in 8,864 (ms)
```

**[2021-08-30T18:36:53.102-0400] [] [INFO] [] [com.ensode.cdiscopes. CdiService] [tid: _ThreadID=76 _ThreadName=http-thread-pool::http- listener(1)] [timeMillis: 1630363013102] [levelValue: 800] init() method called**

```
[2021-08-30T18:36:53.102-0400] [] [INFO] [] [com.ensode.cdiscopes.
CdiService] [tid: _ThreadID=76 _ThreadName=http-thread-pool::http-
listener(1)] [timeMillis: 1630363013102] [levelValue: 800] HTTP POST
request received
```

[2021-08-30T18:36:53.111-0400] [] [INFO] [] **[com.ensode.cdiscopes. CdiService] [tid: _ThreadID=76 _ThreadName=http-thread-pool::http- listener(1)] [timeMillis: 1630363013111] [levelValue: 800] cleanup() method called**

As we can see from the output, both our init() and cleanup() methods were called when we sent an HTTP POST request to our service, as expected; since the service is a request scoped CDI bean, the class was constructed just before servicing the request and then destroyed right after. Payara Micro invoked the method annotated with @PostConstruct right after the bean was instantiated, and the method annotated with @PreDestroy just before the bean was destroyed. In other words, everything worked as expected.

# Dependency Injection

As previously mentioned, we can turn almost any plain old Java object (POJO) into a CDI bean by annotating it with one of the CDI scope annotations.

The following class is an application scoped CDI bean:

```
package com.ensode.dependencyinjection;

//imports omitted

@ApplicationScoped
public class CountryLookup {

  private List<Country> countryList;
  private Map<String, Country> countryMap;

  @PostConstruct
  public void init() {
    countryList = new ArrayList<>();
    countryMap = new HashMap<>();

    countryList.add(new Country("AU", "AUSTRALIA"));
    countryList.add(new Country("UK", "United Kingdom"));
    countryList.add(new Country("IN", "India"));
    countryList.add(new Country("US", "United States"));
    countryList.add(new Country("MX", "Mexico"));
    countryList.add(new Country("EG", "Egypt"));

    countryList.forEach(c -> countryMap.put(
      c.getAbbreviation(), c));
  }

  public Country getCountry(String countryAbbrev) {
    return countryMap.get(countryAbbrev);
  }
}
```

All we had to do to turn the class into a CDI bean was to annotate it with
`@ApplicationScoped`; recall from our previous discussion that application scoped
CDI beans live throughout the lifetime of our application, they are initialized when
the application starts (or, more likely, lazily the first time they are used), and they are
destroyed when we undeploy our application or shut down Payara Micro (or whichever
MicroProfile implementation we may be using).

Application scoped CDI beans are frequently used to cache data that may not change
frequently; this is done for performance purposes to avoid hitting the database every
time the data is needed.

Our application scoped managed bean has a `public void init()` method
annotated with `@PostConstruct`; this annotation causes the method to be invoked
automatically when the bean is constructed by CDI. In our example, the `init()` method
initializes the data to be cached. In a production application, our `init()` method
would probably retrieve the data from a database; in our simple example, we are simply
initializing our data in place.

Our `init()` method creates a `HashMap` in which the keys are of type `String`; they
represent a country abbreviation; the values are instances of a class called `Country`, which
contains two properties: the country abbreviation and the full name of the country.

---

The `Country` class is so simple that we will not show its source; refer to the code
download for this book for the complete source code for our example application.

---

Our application scoped bean also provides a method called `getCountry()` that takes
a `String` containing the country abbreviation and returns the corresponding instance of
the `Country` class.

Since our `CodeLookup` class is a CDI bean, it can be injected not only into other CDI
beans but also to any class managed by Payara Micro. Classes annotated with the `@Path`
annotation are managed by the runtime; therefore, CDI beans can be injected into them.
The following RESTful web service leverages the `CodeLookup` class to look up country
objects from their abbreviation:

```
package com.ensode.dependencyinjection;

//imports omitted

@Path("cdiservice")
```

```
public class CdiService {

    @Inject
    private CountryLookup countryLookup;

    private static final Logger LOGGER = Logger.getLogger(CdiService.class.
    getName());

    @GET
    @Produces(MediaType.APPLICATION_JSON)
    public Country handleGetRequest(
        @QueryParam("countryAbbrev") String countryAbbrev) {
        return countryLookup.getCountry(countryAbbrev);
    }

}
```

Notice that our RESTful web service is not a CDI bean, but since its life cycle is managed by the MicroProfile runtime, we can inject CDI beans into it. In our example, we inject an instance of the CountryLookup class discussed previously. We then implement a method that responds to HTTP GET requests by annotating the method with the @GET annotation; we have the method accept a query parameter called countryAbbrev, which we achieve by annotating the sole method argument with the @QueryParam annotation. Our method body simply invokes the getCountry() method we implemented in our application scoped bean, passing the abbreviation it received as a parameter; since we annotated the method with the @Produces annotation indicating that the method returns data in JSON format, the Country instance returned by the method is automatically converted to a JSON string, which is then returned as the body of the response sent to the client.

We run our service as usual via the Payara Micro Maven plug-in; then we can invoke our endpoint, with the most straightforward way being the curl command-line utility.

```
curl http://localhost:8080/dependency-injection/webresources/
cdiservice?countryAbbrev=AU
```

We should immediately see the output of our RESTful web service invocation on the console, which, unsurprisingly, is a JSON representation of the instance of the Country class returned by our method.

```
{"abbreviation":"AU","name":"AUSTRALIA"}
```

We have just finished covering the two CDI features that give the API its name; scope annotations are the "Contexts" in "Contexts and Dependency Injection"; the @Inject annotation provides the "Dependency Injection" part of CDI. Another CDI feature is an event mechanism, which allows us to implement loosely coupled applications.

# CDI Events

CDI events allow us to loosely couple different parts of our application. One of our classes may fire an event, which is then handled by one or more event listeners. The class firing the event has no knowledge about the listeners; it just fires the event and CDI takes over, invoking listener methods on all event listeners.

## Firing Events

CDI provides the Event class, which is used to fire events; this class uses generics to indicate the event type. The type can be any valid Java type; it could be an instance of java.lang.String, for example, or any plain old Java object (POJO). The following example illustrates how to fire a CDI event:

```java
package com.ensode.cdievents;

//imports omitted

@Path("countryservice")
public class CountryService {

  @Inject
  Event<Country> countryEvent;

  @Inject
  private CountryLookup countryLookup;

  @GET
  @Produces(MediaType.APPLICATION_JSON)
  public Country handleGetRequest(@QueryParam("countryAbbrev") String
  countryAbbrev) {
    return countryLookup.getCountry(countryAbbrev);
  }
```

```
@PUT
@Consumes(MediaType.APPLICATION_JSON)
public void updateCountry(Country country) {
  countryEvent.fire(country);
}

}
```

A class that needs to fire a CDI event needs to have an instance of the CDI provided Event class injected into it; we inject this dependency via the @Inject annotation as usual. The parameterized type of the Event class indicates the type of event being fired. In this case, we are using a simple plain old Java object representing a country; this Country class has two properties: country abbreviation and country full name.

To actually fire the event, we invoke the fire() method on the injected instance of the Event class; this method takes an instance of the generic type indicated in the declaration of our event (an instance of our Country class, in our case).

Notice in our example code, there is no reference whatsoever to the listeners for the event. Our RESTful web service has no information about the listeners at all; it doesn't know what classes listen for this event, or how many listeners there are, or anything else; it simply fires the event and CDI takes over.

## Listening for Events

To listen for events, a CDI bean must implement a public void method taking a single parameter of the type of event it listens to (an instance of the Country class, in our case); this parameter must be annotated with the CDI @Observes annotation. The following code example illustrates the process of listening to CDI events:

```
package com.ensode.cdievents;

//imports omitted

@ApplicationScoped
public class CountryEventLogger {

  private static final Logger LOGGER =
    Logger.getLogger(CountryEventLogger.class.getName());

  public void logCountryEvent(@Observes Country country) {
```

```
    LOGGER.log(Level.INFO, String.format(
      "Event fired for the following country: %s",
      country.getName()));
  }

}
```

In this example, we have an application scoped CDI bean listening for events of instances of the Country class; our example simply sends an entry to the Payara log, indicating the name of the country for which the event was fired.

We can run our example by invoking the usual Maven goals:

```
mvn war:exploded payara-micro:start
```

Toward the end of the Payara Micro output, we see some information about the deployed RESTful web service endpoints.

```
Payara Micro URLs:
http://192.168.1.165:8080/cdi-events

'cdi-events-1.0-SNAPSHOT' REST Endpoints:
GET /cdi-events/webresources/application.wadl
GET /cdi-events/webresources/countryservice
PUT /cdi-events/webresources/countryservice

]]
```

In our example, the relevant endpoint accepts an HTTP PUT request; we can invoke it via the curl command-line utility.

```
curl -X PUT http://localhost:8080/cdi-events/webresources/countryservice
-H "Content-Type: application/json" --data '{"abbreviation":"TS","name":"
Test"}'
```

In the preceding example, we are passing a JSON string as the request body, passing a (obviously fictitious) test country to our RESTful web service endpoint. When our RESTful web service endpoint receives the request, since the JSON string we passed as the request body conforms to the structure of the JSON class, it automatically populates an instance of this class with the data we passed. Our method then simply fires an event with this populated object, our listener then is invoked by CDI, and its method listening for the event is automatically executed. If we look at the output for Payara Micro, we can see the expected log file entry.

```
[2021-09-03T15:06:54.464-0400] [] [INFO] [] [com.ensode.cdievents.
CountryEventLogger] [tid: _ThreadID=78 _ThreadName=http-thread-pool::http-
listener(1)] [timeMillis: 1630696014464] [levelValue: 800] Event fired for
the following country: Test
```

As we can see, it is fairly easy for us as application developers to implement event handling in CDI applications, as all the heavy lifting is taken care of by CDI; all we need to do is add a couple of annotations (@Inject, @Observable) and call a single method (Event.fire()); everything else is taken care of behind the scenes.

What we just explained works great if there is a single event for a given type, but what if we need to fire more than one event for the same type? How would the event listeners know which event to listen for? This is where CDI qualifiers enter the picture.

# Qualifiers

CDI qualifiers are Java annotations that they themselves are annotated with the CDI @Qualifier annotation. We write qualifiers when we need to differentiate between objects of the same type but used for different purposes. When dealing with CDI events, we use qualifiers when we need to fire more than one event of the same type.

For example, let's say we needed to fire an event when a Country was added or updated; we could create an @Updated qualifier so that we could create an event to be fired only when one of these actions is performed.

```
package com.ensode.cdievents.qualifier;

//imports omitted

@Qualifier
@Retention(RetentionPolicy.RUNTIME)
@Target({ElementType.FIELD, ElementType.PARAMETER})
public @interface Updated {
}
```

As we can see, our qualifier is a standard Java annotation to be processed at runtime, as specified by the @Retention(RetentionPolicy.RUNTIME) annotation. Qualifiers for CDI events are applied when we declare the instance of the Event class and on the corresponding parameter of any listener method; therefore, we specify `ElementType.FIELD` and `ElementType.PARAMETER` as the values of the `@Target` annotation for our qualifier.

Suppose then that we needed to fire a different Country event when a country was deleted; for this, we would use another qualifier.

```
package com.ensode.cdievents.qualifier;

//imports omitted

@Qualifier
@Retention(RetentionPolicy.RUNTIME)
@Target({ElementType.FIELD, ElementType.PARAMETER})
public @interface Deleted {
}
```

We can now apply these qualifiers to differentiate different types of events for the Country class.

```
package com.ensode.cdievents;

//imports omitted

@Path("countryservice")
public class CountryService {

  @Inject
  private @Updated Event<Country> countryEvent;

  @Inject
  private @Deleted Event<Country> countryDeletedEvent;

  @Inject
  private CountryLookup countryLookup;

  @GET
  @Produces(MediaType.APPLICATION_JSON)
  public Country handleGetRequest(
    @QueryParam("countryAbbrev") String countryAbbrev) {
    return countryLookup.getCountry(countryAbbrev);
  }
```

```
@PUT
@Consumes(MediaType.APPLICATION_JSON)
public void updateCountry(Country country) {
  countryEvent.fire(country);
}

@DELETE
@Consumes(MediaType.APPLICATION_JSON)
public void deleteCountry(
  @QueryParam("countryAbbrev") String countryAbbrev) {
  Country country=countryLookup.getCountry(countryAbbrev);
  countryDeletedEvent.fire(country);
}

}
```

Notice that we updated our RESTful web service; we now declare two instances of Event<Country>; one is meant to be fired when a country is added or updated and the other one when a country is deleted; we decorated each instance with our custom @Updated and @Deleted qualifiers.

In addition to the previously existing updateCountry() method, we added a new deleteCountry() method; this method will be invoked when our service receives an HTTP DELETE request, as specified by the @DELETE annotation. This new method fires the second instance of the Country event we added to our service so that listeners can perform any necessary logic when a country is deleted.

On the listener side, we need to use the same qualifier on the corresponding listener method. Let's take a look at a CDI event listener with two listener methods, one for each type of event.

```
package com.ensode.cdievents;

//imports omitted

@ApplicationScoped
public class CountryManager {

  private static final Logger LOGGER = Logger.getLogger(CountryManager.
  class.getName());
```

```
@Inject
private CountryLookup countryLookup;

public void updateCountry(@Observes @Updated Country country) {
  LOGGER.log(Level.INFO, String.format("Updating the following country:
  %s", country.getName()));
  countryLookup.updateCountry(country);
}

public void deleteCountry(@Observes @Deleted Country country) {
  LOGGER.log(Level.INFO, String.format("Deleting the following country:
  %s", country.getName()));
  countryLookup.deleteCountry(country);
}
}
```

As we can see, on the listener side, we use our qualifiers to indicate which event will be handled by each listener method. If we don't specify a qualifier on the listener, then the method will handle all events corresponding to the Country class.

We can send an HTTP PUT request to our service via curl as before:

```
curl -X PUT http://localhost:8080/cdi-events/webresources/countryservice -H
"Content-Type: application/json" --data '{"abbreviation":"TS","name":"
Test"}'
```

If we inspect Payara Micro's output, we can see the log entries generated by the listener:

```
[2021-09-07T08:46:39.610-0400] [] [INFO] [] [com.ensode.cdievents.
CountryEventLogger] [tid: _ThreadID=76 _ThreadName=http-thread-pool::http-
listener(1)] [timeMillis: 1631018799610] [levelValue: 800] Event fired for
the following country: Test
```

```
[2021-09-07T08:46:39.610-0400] [] [INFO] [] [com.ensode.cdievents.
CountryManager] [tid: _ThreadID=76 _ThreadName=http-thread-pool::http-
listener(1)] [timeMillis: 1631018799610] [levelValue: 800] Updating the
following country: Test
```

Notice that our previous listener was invoked; since its argument doesn't have a qualifier, it gets invoked for every event of any instance of the Country class. Additionally, we can see that the listener method with the @Updated qualifier was invoked; this happens because the HTTP PUT request caused the @PUT annotated `updateCountry()` method in our service to be invoked, which fires an event of Country with the `@Updated` qualifier. Unsurprisingly, the listener method listening for Country events with the `@Deleted` qualifier wasn't invoked; for this, we need to send an HTTP DELETE request to the service.

```
curl  -X DELETE http://localhost:8080/cdi-events/webresources/countryservic
e?countryAbbrev=TS
```

When we inspect the Payara Micro output, we can see that the appropriate event listener methods were invoked.

```
[2021-09-07T08:59:31.208-0400] [] [INFO] [] [com.ensode.cdievents.
CountryEventLogger] [tid: _ThreadID=76 _ThreadName=http-thread-pool::http-
listener(1)] [timeMillis: 1631019571208] [levelValue: 800] Event fired for
the following country: Test

[2021-09-07T08:59:31.209-0400] [] [INFO] [] [com.ensode.cdievents.
CountryManager] [tid: _ThreadID=76 _ThreadName=http-thread-pool::http-
listener(1)] [timeMillis: 1631019571209] [levelValue: 800] Deleting the
following country: Test
```

As expected, both the unqualified event listener method and the event method qualified with @Deleted were invoked.

## Observing CDI Scopes

In addition to allowing us to create custom event types via qualifiers, CDI includes a few built-in qualifiers that allow us to implement some logic whenever a CDI scope is initialized or destroyed.

These qualifiers take a class parameter indicating the CDI scope they will listen for; for example, to have a listener invoked when the application scope is initialized, we would use code similar to the following:

```
public void applicationScopeInitListener(@Observes
@Initialized(ApplicationScoped.class) Object object){
  //actual logic goes here
}
```

We need to have a parameter in the listener of type object, just because it needs to be annotated with the @Observes and @Initialized annotations; we don't actually need to use the parameter in the body of our method. The @Destroyed and @BeforeDestroyed qualifiers follow the same pattern; @BeforeDestroyed causes a listener method to be invoked just before a CDI scope is destroyed; @Destroyed results in a listener method being invoked right after a scope is destroyed.

Table 4-2 lists the types to use as parameters to @Initialized, @Destroyed, and @BeforeDestroyed for each CDI scope.

***Table 4-2.*** *CDI Scope Classes*

| CDI Scope | Type |
| --- | --- |
| Request | RequestScoped.class |
| Session | SessionScoped.class |
| Application | ApplicationScoped.class |

Notice that the types correspond to the annotations used when declaring the scope for a CDI bean.

Listening for application scope initialization allows us to perform some code just before our application executes. It is possible to write "command-line" applications with the full power of MicroProfile and Jakarta EE APIs with this. A frequently used trick is to write RESTful web service clients using the MicroProfile RESTful client API from a listener method. The following example illustrates how to do this:

```
package com.ensode.cdievents.client;

//imports omitted
@ApplicationScoped
public class CountryServiceClient {

  private static final Logger LOGGER = Logger.
  getLogger(CountryServiceClient.class.getName());

  @Inject
  @RestClient
```

```
private CountryService cdiService;

public void updateCountries(
  @Observes @Initialized(ApplicationScoped.class) Object o) {
  Country testCountry = new Country("TS", "Test");
  Country albanya = new Country("AL", "Albanya");
  Country albania = new Country("AL", "Albania");

  cdiService.updateCountry(testCountry);
  cdiService.deleteCountry(testCountry.getAbbreviation());
  cdiService.updateCountry(albanya);
  cdiService.updateCountry(albania);
  }
}
```

In this example, we have an application scoped bean with a listener method containing the @Observes and @Initialized(ApplicationScoped.class), which causes the method to be invoked when the application scope is initialized. Since our class is an application scoped CDI bean, we can inject a RESTful web service client interface into it via the @Inject and @RestClient annotations.

---

As you may recall from our discussion of the MicroProfile RESTful client API, a RESTful client interface is a Java interface containing method signatures matching those of the corresponding RESTful web service.

---

In our client, we simply initialize a POJO to be passed to the client, which is converted to a JSON string by the MicroProfile runtime and passed as the body of the request to our service, or pass any required query or path parameters to our method.

We can run our client as usual with the help of the Maven WAR and Payara Micro plug-ins:

```
mvn war:exploded payara-micro:start
```

After running our client, we can see the expected output in the Payara Micro output for the service.

```
[2021-09-08T10:18:37.083-0400] [] [INFO] [] [com.ensode.cdievents.
CountryEventLogger] [tid: _ThreadID=78 _ThreadName=http-thread-pool::http-
listener(2)] [timeMillis: 1631110717083] [levelValue: 800] Event fired for
the following country: Test

[2021-09-08T10:18:37.084-0400] [] [INFO] [] [com.ensode.cdievents.
CountryManager] [tid: _ThreadID=78 _ThreadName=http-thread-pool::http-
listener(2)] [timeMillis: 1631110717084] [levelValue: 800] Updating the
following country: Test

[2021-09-08T10:18:37.117-0400] [] [INFO] [] [com.ensode.cdievents.
CountryEventLogger] [tid: _ThreadID=77 _ThreadName=http-thread-pool::http-
listener(1)] [timeMillis: 1631110717117] [levelValue: 800] Event fired for
the following country: Test

[2021-09-08T10:18:37.118-0400] [] [INFO] [] [com.ensode.cdievents.
CountryManager] [tid: _ThreadID=77 _ThreadName=http-thread-pool::http-
listener(1)] [timeMillis: 1631110717118] [levelValue: 800] Deleting the
following country: Test

[2021-09-08T10:18:37.125-0400] [] [INFO] [] [com.ensode.cdievents.
CountryEventLogger] [tid: _ThreadID=78 _ThreadName=http-thread-pool::http-
listener(2)] [timeMillis: 1631110717125] [levelValue: 800] Event fired for
the following country: Albanya

[2021-09-08T10:18:37.126-0400] [] [INFO] [] [com.ensode.cdievents.
CountryManager] [tid: _ThreadID=78 _ThreadName=http-thread-pool::http-
listener(2)] [timeMillis: 1631110717126] [levelValue: 800] Updating the
following country: Albanya

[2021-09-08T10:18:37.132-0400] [] [INFO] [] [com.ensode.cdievents.
CountryEventLogger] [tid: _ThreadID=77 _ThreadName=http-thread-pool::http-
listener(1)] [timeMillis: 1631110717132] [levelValue: 800] Event fired for
the following country: Albania
```

```
[2021-09-08T10:18:37.132-0400] [] [INFO] [] [com.ensode.cdievents.
CountryManager] [tid: _ThreadID=77 _ThreadName=http-thread-pool::http-
listener(1)] [timeMillis: 1631110717132] [levelValue: 800] Updating the
following country: Albania
```

Writing "command-line" RESTful web service clients this way is a neat way to test our web services without us having to come up with the proper JSON strings to pass to the service, leaving MicroProfile to do the tedious work for us.

# Summary

In this chapter, we covered the Contexts and Dependency Injection API available to us in our Payara Micro MicroProfile and Jakarta EE applications. We saw how we can assign a scope to CDI managed beans and how to perform logic on bean initialization or destruction.

Additionally, we covered how we can easily inject CDI beans via the @Inject annotation into any object managed by Payara Micro, such as RESTful web services, or other CDI beans.

We also explained the CDI event handling mechanism, which allows us to write loosely coupled applications. We covered how to use CDI events to write application logic when a CDI scope is initialized or destroyed, then used this newfound knowledge for a neat trick that allowed us to execute logic as soon as our WAR file is deployed, and then exploited this knowledge to develop command-line RESTful web service clients using the MicroProfile RESTful web service API.

# CHAPTER 5

# Application Configuration

MicroProfile includes a configuration API called, appropriately enough, MicroProfile Config that standardizes the way we can configure our applications. Configuration is used to set values that may vary from environment to environment, for example, things like database URLs or directories in a file system. MicroProfile Config standardizes the way we retrieve properties to retrieve configuration values for our applications.

## Configuration Sources

There are three standard ways we can configure our applications: via a *microprofile-config.properties* file inside our WAR file, via Java system properties, and via environment variables. We can also add our own custom configuration sources.

Configuration sources have priorities defined by their *ordinal values*; higher ordinal values have priority over lower ones. Table 5-1 summarizes the ordinal values of all standard configuration sources.

***Table 5-1.*** *MicroProfile Config Sources Default Ordinal Values*

| Configuration Source | Default Ordinal Value |
|---|---|
| microprofile-config.properties | 100 |
| Environment variables | 300 |
| System Properties | 400 |

In addition to the standard MicroProfile Config configuration sources, Payara Micro implements a number of additional configuration sources we can use to configure our applications (discussed later in the chapter). Table 5-2 lists all Payara Micro–specific configuration sources, along with their default ordinal value.

63

© David R. Heffelfinger 2022
D. R. Heffelfinger, *Payara Micro Revealed*, https://doi.org/10.1007/978-1-4842-8161-1_5

**Table 5-2.**  *Payara Micro Configuration*
*Sources Default Ordinal Values*

| Configuration Source | Default Ordinal Value |
|---|---|
| Directory | 90 |
| Password | 105 |
| Domain | 110 |
| JNDI | 115 |
| Config | 120 |
| Server | 130 |
| Application | 140 |
| Module | 150 |
| Cluster | 160 |
| JDBC | 190 |
| LDAP | 200 |
| Cloud provider specific | 180 |

Default ordinal values can be overridden by adding a `config_ordinal` property to the configuration source; for example, if we wanted to increase the ordinal value of *microprofile-config.properties* to be higher than environment variables (which have an ordinal value of 300) but lower than system properties (which have an ordinal value of 400), we could add a property to *microprofile-config.properties* containing a value between their ordinal values, for example:

`config_ordinal=350`

As we can see, *microprofile-config.properties* has the lowest ordinal value of the standard configuration sources; this is useful for when we want to include default configuration values packaged within our application, which can then be easily overridden by setting the appropriate environment variable or system property.

Please note that the API to retrieve properties is exactly the same no matter what configuration source is used; the MicroProfile Config API will look for properties starting with the highest priority source and going down the line to the lowest priority configuration source until it finds a matching property name.

# Configuration via Property Files

The easiest and most straightforward way to configure our applications is by adding *microprofile-config.properties* file to our WAR file; the standard location for this file is inside the META-INF directory at the root of the CLASSPATH of our WAR files. In a typical Maven project, the location of the property file in the WAR file would be *WEB-INF/classes/META-INF/microprofile-config.properties*; on the source code, we would place it under *src/main/resources/META-INF/microprofile-config.properties*, with Maven placing the file in the correct location in the WAR file when we build our code.

To see an example of this, let's suppose we want to send additional output to the Payara Micro log when we are in a development environment but suppress that output in other environments such as test or production. To accomplish something like this, we could set a `project.stage` property in *microprofile-config.properties*.

```
project.stage=production
```

In a standard Maven project, this file needs to be placed under *src/resources/META-INF*. Figure 5-1 illustrates the directory tree.

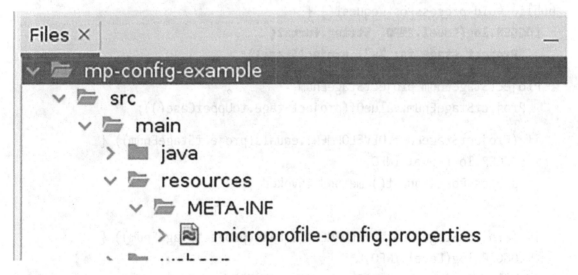

***Figure 5-1.*** *microprofile-config.properties directory location*

We can retrieve the property via the @ConfigProperty annotation provided by the MicroProfile Config API.

```
package com.ensode.mp.config.example;

//imports omitted

@RequestScoped
@Path("mpconfigexample")
public class MpConfigDemoService {

  private static final Logger LOGGER =
    Logger.getLogger(MpConfigDemoService.class.getName());

  @Inject
  @ConfigProperty(name = "project.stage")
  private String projectStage;

  @POST
  @Produces(MediaType.APPLICATION_JSON)
  public void processPostRequest() {
    LOGGER.log(Level.INFO, String.format(
      "Project stage is: %s", projectStage));

    ProjectStageEnum projectStageEnum =
      ProjectStageEnum.valueOf(projectStage.toUpperCase());

    if (ProjectStageEnum.DEVELOPMENT.equals(projectStageEnum)) {
      LOGGER.log(Level.INFO,
      "processPostRequest() method invoked");
    }

    if (ProjectStageEnum.DEVELOPMENT.equals(projectStageEnum)) {
      LOGGER.log(Level.INFO,
        "leaving processPostRequest() method");
    }

  }

}
```

As we can see in the example, we need to use CDI's @Inject annotation in conjunction with @ConfigProperty to retrieve the value of the property. @ConfigProperty has a name attribute whose value needs to match the name of the property as defined in *microprofile-config.properties*.

When developing our applications, the easiest and most straightforward way to run our code is via Maven, as usual.

```
mvn war:exploded payara-micro:start
```

We can send an HTTP POST request using *curl* as follows:

```
curl -X POST http://localhost:8080/mpconfigex/webresources/mpconfigexample
```

After doing so, we examine Payara Micro's output and see that, as expected, no additional output was logged, since we set the project.stage property to production.

```
[2021-09-15T08:08:41.306-0400] [] [INFO] [] [PayaraMicro] [tid: _ThreadID=1
_ThreadName=main] [timeMillis: 1631707721306] [levelValue: 800] Payara
Micro  5.2021.6 #badassmicrofish (build 4579) ready in 8,542 (ms)
```

```
[2021-09-15T08:08:48.085-0400] [] [INFO] [] [com.ensode.mp.config.example.
MpConfigDemoService] [tid: _ThreadID=78 _ThreadName=http-thread pool::http-
listener(2)] [timeMillis: 1631707728085] [levelValue: 800] Project stage
is: production
```

```
[2021-09-15T08:33:14.192-0400] [] [INFO] [] [fish.payara.micro.cdi.
extension.ClusteredCDIEventBusImpl] [tid: _ThreadID=83 _ThreadName=payara-
executor-service-scheduled-task] [timeMillis: 1631709194192] [levelValue:
800] Clustered CDI Event bus initialized
```

We can change the value of the property to development by modifying *microprofile-config.properties*.

```
project.stage=development
```

We re-run our application and send another POST request; this time additional output is sent to the Payara Micro log.

```
[2021-09-15T08:45:42.535-0400] [] [INFO] [] [com.ensode.mp.config.example.
MpConfigDemoService] [tid: _ThreadID=76 _ThreadName=http-thread-pool::http-
listener(2)] [timeMillis: 1631709942535] [levelValue: 800] Project stage
is: development
```

```
[2021-09-15T08:45:42.537-0400] [] [INFO] [] [com.ensode.mp.config.
example.MpConfigDemoService] [tid: _ThreadID=76 _ThreadName=http-thread-
pool::http-listener(2)] [timeMillis: 1631709942537] [levelValue: 800]
processPostRequest() method invoked
```

```
[2021-09-15T08:45:42.537-0400] [] [INFO] [] [com.ensode.mp.config.example.
MpConfigDemoService] [tid: _ThreadID=76 _ThreadName=http-thread-pool::http-
listener(2)] [timeMillis: 1631709942537] [levelValue: 800] leaving
processPostRequest() method
```

Reading a configuration property via the @ConfigProperty annotation is simple and straightforward; however, it isn't very flexible; it is possible that the property we are attempting to read may not exist when our application is deployed, in which case we would get an exception; additionally, there is no way to conditionally assign the value of a property to a variable. To cover these use cases and provide more flexibility, MicroProfile Config provides a Config class that can be used to programmatically retrieve property values. The following example illustrates its usage:

```
package com.ensode.mp.config.example;

//imports omitted

@RequestScoped
@Path("mpconfigexample")
public class MpConfigDemoService {

  private static final Logger LOGGER = Logger.
  getLogger(MpConfigDemoService.class.getName());

  @Inject
  private Config config;

  private String projectStage;

  @POST
  @Produces(MediaType.APPLICATION_JSON)
  public void processPostRequest() {
```

```
projectStage = config.getValue("project.stage", String.class);

LOGGER.log(Level.INFO, String.format("Project stage is: %s",
projectStage));

ProjectStageEnum projectStageEnum = ProjectStageEnum.
valueOf(projectStage.toUpperCase());

if (ProjectStageEnum.DEVELOPMENT.equals(projectStageEnum)) {
  LOGGER.log(Level.INFO, "processPostRequest() method invoked");
}

if (ProjectStageEnum.DEVELOPMENT.equals(projectStageEnum)) {
  LOGGER.log(Level.INFO, "leaving processPostRequest() method");
}

  }

}
```

Here, we modified our previous example to use the Config class; as we can see, Config can be injected via the CDI @Inject annotation; we can then retrieve a property value via its getValue() method, its first argument being a String containing the property name we wish to retrieve and the second value being the type of the property value variable. In our case, we are assigning the property to a String; therefore, we use String.class as the second argument to Config.getValue(); had we been retrieving an integer numerical value for example, we would use Integer.class as the second argument to Config.getValue().

---

We can also obtain an instance of Config by invoking ConfigProvider.getConfig(), but injecting via CDI is easier and more straightforward.

---

We have now seen how to retrieve properties from the standard *microprofile-config. property* file; as we can see, this approach to configuration is simple and straightforward; however, if we need to change the value of a property, the file needs to be modified, and our code rebuilt and redeployed. In our example, we would need different versions of the property file for different environments (development, test, production, etc.). For this reason, it is sometimes desirable to have configuration information outside of our deployment module. The MicroProfile Config specification defines two ways we can accomplish this: retrieving properties via environment variables and via Java System properties; we discuss these approaches next.

## Configuration via Environment Variables

All modern operating systems allow us to define environment variables that can be read by processes running on the operating system.

For example, in the Unix BASH shell, we could define an environment variable as follows:

```
$ export PROJECT_STAGE=test
```

This would define an environment variable named PROJECT_STAGE with a value of "test".

MicroProfile Config can read environment variables and retrieve their values; the following example illustrates how to do that:

```
package com.ensode.mp.config.example;

//imports omitted

@RequestScoped
@Path("mpconfigexample")
public class MpConfigDemoService {

  private static final Logger LOGGER = Logger.
  getLogger(MpConfigDemoService.class.getName());

  @Inject
  @ConfigProperty(name = "PROJECT_STAGE")
  private String projectStage;

  @POST
  @Produces(MediaType.APPLICATION_JSON)
  public void processPostRequest() {
    LOGGER.log(Level.INFO, String.format("Project stage is: %s",
    projectStage));

    ProjectStageEnum projectStageEnum =
      ProjectStageEnum.valueOf(projectStage.toUpperCase());
```

```
    if (ProjectStageEnum.DEVELOPMENT.equals(projectStageEnum)) {
      LOGGER.log(Level.INFO,
      "processPostRequest() method invoked");
    }

    if (ProjectStageEnum.DEVELOPMENT.equals(projectStageEnum)) {
      LOGGER.log(Level.INFO,
      "leaving processPostRequest() method");
    }

  }

}
```

Notice that the only thing we changed from our previous example was the property name in the @ConfigProperty annotation; everything else is exactly the same. The MicroProfile Config API is exactly the same no matter what configuration source we are using, which is very convenient as we don't need to modify our code if we change the source of our properties.

---

In our example, we used the @ConfigSource annotation to retrieve the environment variable value; Config.getValue() would have worked just as well.

---

It is also worth pointing out that no special configuration is needed; we simply set the environment variable on our operating system shell and run our code; MicroProfile Config will read the environment variable without additional effort on our part.

## Configuration via System Properties

The Java Virtual Machine (JVM) has a number of built-in system properties we can use to retrieve information about the environment we are working on. It has properties indicating things like the Java version we are using (java.version), the user's home directory (home.dir), and many others. We can also add our own system properties programmatically or via the command line.

As previously mentioned, the MicroProfile Config API for retrieving property values is the same no matter what configuration source we are using; using system properties as a configuration source is no exception.

We can pass a system property to the JVM running Payara Micro by configuring the Payara Micro Maven plug-in:

```
<plugin>
        <groupId>fish.payara.maven.plugins</groupId>
        <artifactId>payara-micro-maven-plugin</artifactId>
        <version>1.4.0</version>
        <configuration>
          <payaraVersion>${version.payara}</payaraVersion>
          <javaCommandLineOptions>
          <option>
            <key>-Dmy.system.property</key>
            <value>
              "If you don't see this, it didn't work"
            </value>
          </option>
        </javaCommandLineOptions>
        <deployWar>false</deployWar>
        <commandLineOptions>
          <option>
            <key>--autoBindHttp</key>
          </option>
          <option>
            <key>--deploy</key>
            <value>${project.build.directory}/${project.build.
            finalName}</value>
          </option>
        </commandLineOptions>
        <contextRoot>/mpconfigex</contextRoot>
      </configuration>
    </plugin>
```

In general, the `<javaCommandLineOptions>` tag of the Payara Micro Maven plug-in allows us to pass arguments to the JVM; in this particular case, we are setting a system property so that it is available to the MicroProfile Config API.

When running Payara Micro from the command line, we can pass a system property to the JVM as follows:

```
java -Dmy.system.property="If you don't see this, it didn't work" -jar
~/.m2/repository/fish/payara/extras/payara-micro/5.2021.7/payara-
micro-5.2021.7.jar --deploy ./target/mp-config-example-1.0-SNAPSHOT.
war:mpconfigex
```

> So far, we've only discussed running Payara Micro from the Maven plug-in; the preceding example starts Payara Micro directly from the command line; we will cover various ways of starting Payara Micro in Chapter 12.

We can then read the system property as usual, either by using the @ConfigSource annotation or via Config.getValue().

```
@Inject
@ConfigProperty(name = "my.system.property")
private String sysPropVal;
```

Then we can use the property value as usual.

# Payara Specific Config Sources

Payara Micro includes additional configuration sources on top of the ones defined by the MicroProfile Config specification.

```
https://docs.payara.fish/enterprise/docs/5.25.0/documentation/
microprofile/config.html
```

## Directory Configuration Source

Payara Micro can read the files in a directory and use the file names as property names, with their contents as the values.

> The directory configuration source can be used to read Kubernetes secrets files.

For example, let's suppose we had a directory /tmp/props_dir in our file system, and we wish the file names in the directory to be used as property names for MicroProfile Config, with their contents being the corresponding property values. Figure 5-2 illustrates the directory structure in a typical Linux terminal.

**Figure 5-2.** *Sample directory for the directory configuration source*

We need to configure Payara Micro to specify the directory containing the files to be used as properties. Using Payara Server, this is typically done via the `asadmin` command-line utility. This utility is not included with Payara Micro; however, we can pass `asadmin` commands to Payara Micro via a text file and the `–postbootcommandfile` file command-line argument.

For example, let's say we had a text file named *post-boot-commands.txt* with the following contents:

```
set-config-dir –directory=/tmp/props_dir
```

set-config-dir is an asadmin command to specify the directory in the file system to be used as a configuration source; the path to the directory is specified as the value of the -directory argument to set-config-dir.

We can then tell Payara Micro to read this file by passing the –postbootcommandfile parameter as follows:

```
java -jar path/to/payara-micro.jar --deploy path/to/warfile.war
--postbootcommandfile=/tmp/props_dir
```

When using the Payara Micro Maven plug-in, we can place the file in src/main/ resources and configure the plug-in as follows:

```
<plugin>
        <groupId>fish.payara.maven.plugins</groupId>
        <artifactId>payara-micro-maven-plugin</artifactId>
        <version>1.4.0</version>
        <configuration>
          <payaraVersion>${version.payara}</payaraVersion>
          <deployWar>false</deployWar>
          <commandLineOptions>
            <option>
              <key>--postbootcommandfile</key>
              <value>
              ${basedir}/src/main/resources/post-boot-commands.txt
              </value>
            </option>
            <!-- other command line options omitted -->
          </commandLineOptions>
          <contextRoot>/mpconfigex</contextRoot>
        </configuration>
      </plugin>
```

Configuring the plug-in this way allows us to configure Payara Micro when we wish to run via the payara-micro:start Maven goal.

Once we have configured the directory configuration source, we can retrieve property values as usual; for example, using the @ConfigProperty annotation, we could retrieve the contents of one of the files in the directory as follows:

```
@Inject
@ConfigProperty(name = "file1")
private String value;
```

This would read the contents of the file named *file1* in the configuration directory and assign its contents to the annotated value variable.

## Password Configuration Source

Both Payara Server and Payara Micro allow us to set up password aliases. The purpose of password aliases is security; password aliases allow us to use an alias instead of actual passwords whenever we need to read a password. This prevents us from having to hard-code passwords in our code.

In order to set a password alias in Payara Micro, we need to create a password file with the desired password, as follows:

```
AS_ADMIN_ALIASPASSWORD=secret
```

Then we use the create-password-alias command in the post boot command file:

```
create-password-alias my-password --passwordfile=/path/to/password.txt
```

If we need to create multiple password aliases, we would create multiple password files and have multiple create-password-alias commands in the post boot command file:

```
create-password-alias my-password --passwordfile=/tmp/password.txt
create-password-alias another-password –passwordfile=/tmp/password2.txt
```

Once we have created our password aliases, the property names to retrieve them adhere to the following pattern: ${ALIAS=alias-name}.

In our example post boot command file, we created two password aliases, named *my-password* and *another-password*; we would retrieve those in our code via the @ConfigSource annotation as follows:

```
@Inject
@ConfigProperty(name = "${ALIAS=my-password}")
private String password;
```

```
@Inject
@ConfigProperty(name = "${ALIAS=another-password}")
private String password2;
```

We could, of course, use the equivalent methods in a Config object to retrieve the values as well.

## Domain Configuration Source

Payara Server has a concept of *domains*; we can group deployed applications into a domain, and they would all share common configuration, things like JDBC connection pools, etc. We can set up multiple domains into an instance of Payara Server. Multiple domains are not possible in Payara Micro; however, deployed applications are added to a default domain.

We can add domain properties to Payara Micro via a command file as follows:

```
set-config-property --propertyName=domain.property.name
--propertyValue='some value' –source=domain
```

The property would be added to the default Payara Micro domain and can be retrieved in our code as usual.

```
@Inject
@ConfigProperty(name = "domain.property.name")
private String value;
```

## JNDI Configuration Source

Java Naming and Directory Interface is an API used to look up resources in our applications; for example, things like database connections can be given a JNDI name and retrieved via the JNDI API.

Payara Micro allows us to retrieve JNDI properties via the MicroProfile Config API, via its custom JNDI configuration source.

Before we can retrieve a property via JNDI, we need to set it via a post boot command file:

```
create-custom-resource --restype=string --factoryclass=org.glassfish.
resources.custom.factory.PrimitivesAndStringFactory --property value="jndi-
property-val" jndi-property-name
```

A full explanation on setting JNDI resources is beyond our scope, for our purposes, suffice to say that Payara includes a JNDI factory class that can be used to add JNDI name/value pairs for Java primitives (int, long, float, double, boolean, etc.) and strings. We can use this factory class to create a JNDI name/value pair we can then retrieve via the MicroProfile Config API. In our example command file before, we are setting a property of type String whose name is *jndi-property-name*, and its value is *jndi-property-value*.

We instruct Payara Micro to execute the command file from the command line as usual; then we can retrieve property values set in JNDI from the JNDI configuration source, for example:

```
@Inject
@ConfigProperty(name = "jndi-property-name")
private String propertyVal;
```

## Config Configuration Source

Payara Server has a concept of *named configurations*; different instances of GlassFish in the same domain can have separate configurations. The Payara Micro default domain has a single configuration, named *server-config*. We can add a property to Payara Micro's configuration via a command file as follows:

```
set-config-property --propertyName=my.config.property
--propertyValue='config property value' --source=config
--sourceName=server-config
```

We can then retrieve the value of the property from our code as usual:

```
@Inject
@ConfigProperty(name = "my.config.property")
private String value;
```

## Server Configuration Source

Properties set at the server configuration source will be accessible from a single instance of Payara Micro. We can add properties to the server MicroProfile Config source via a command file as illustrated in the following example.

```
set-config-property --propertyName=my.config.property --propertyValue='from
server source' --source=server –sourceName=server
```

We can then retrieve the property values from our code via the @ConfigSource annotation or by invoking Config.getConfigValue() as usual.

## Application Configuration Source

It is possible to deploy more than one WAR file to a single instance of Payara Micro; we can do this from the command line, simply by adding multiple --deploy arguments to the Payara Micro command line.

```
java -jar pat/to/payara-micro.jar --deploy path/to/mp-config-example-1.0-
SNAPSHOT.war:mpconfigex --deploy path/to/mp-application-config-example-1.0-
SNAPSHOT.war:mpappconfigex
```

In this example, we would deploy two WAR files, one named *mp-config-example-1.0-SNAPSHOT.war* and the other one named *mp-application-config-example-1.0-SNAPSHOT.war*. Each WAR file deployed to Payara Micro is assigned an application name corresponding to the base name of the WAR file (mp-config-example-1.0-SNAPSHOT and mp-application-config-example-1.0-SNAPSHOT in our example). We need to specify the application name when we set the property in the command file, as follows:

```
set-config-property --propertyName=my.config.property --propertyValue='from
application source' --source=application --sourceName=mp-config-
example-1.0-SNAPSHOT
set-config-property --propertyName=my.config.property --propertyValue='A
different value' --source=application –sourceName=mp-application-config-
example-1.0-SNAPSHOT
```

Executing these commands from a command file passed to the postbootcommandfile Payara Micro argument will fail, since the files have not been deployed yet at the time this command is run; thankfully, Payara Micro provides an alternate way to execute commands from a file, via the postdeploycommandfile argument.

```
java -jar path/to/payara-micro.jar --deploy path/to/mp-config-example-1.0-
SNAPSHOT.war:mpconfigex --deploy path/to/mp-application-config-example-1.0-
SNAPSHOT.war:mpappconfigex --postdeploycommandfile src/main/resources/post-
deploy-commands.txt
```

The name of the file can be anything; it just needs to be a plain text file containing *asadmin* commands to pass to Payara Micro.

Commands executed from the postdeploymentcommandfile Payara Micro argument will not be executed until after the WAR files are deployed; therefore, if we are setting MicroProfile Config properties this way, injecting configuration values will fail, since they are not set at the time the application is deployed. In this case, we need to retrieve values via either `Config.getConfigValue()` or `Config.getValue()`.

For example, in one of our WAR files, we could retrieve the value as follows:

```
value = config.getValue("my.config.property", String.class);
```

As previously mentioned, the first argument to `getValue()` is the property name; the second argument is the type of the property we are reading. The following example illustrates how we could retrieve the property value in this manner:

```
package com.ensode.mp.config.example;

//imports omitted

@RequestScoped
@Path("mpconfigexample")
public class MpConfigDemoService {

  private static final Logger LOGGER = Logger.
  getLogger(MpConfigDemoService.class.getName());

  private String value;

  @Inject
  private Config config;

  @POST
  @Produces(MediaType.APPLICATION_JSON)
  public void processPostRequest() {

    value = config.getValue("my.config.property", String.class);

    LOGGER.log(Level.INFO, String.format(
      "Property value is: %s", value));

  }

}
```

This service would display the property value to the Payara Micro log when it receives an HTTP POST request.

Alternatively, we could retrieve the property value via Config.getConfigValue().

```
ConfigValue configValue = config.getConfigValue("my.config.property");
return String.format("Property value is %s", configValue.getValue());
```

Confg.getValue() returns an instance of ConfigValue, which in turn has a getValue() method that returns the property value as a string.

We could have a second RESTful web service, in a different WAR file, that could retrieve the property value in this manner.

```
package com.ensode.mp.application.config.example;

//imports omitted

@RequestScoped
@Path("appconfig")
public class AppconfigResource {

  @Inject
  private Config config;

  @GET
  @Produces(MediaType.TEXT_PLAIN)
  public String processGetRequest() {
    ConfigValue configValue =
      config.getConfigValue("my.config.property");
    return String.format("Property value is %s",
      configValue.getValue());
  }

}
```

This example would return the value of the property as plain text to the client invoking the service.

After setting the properties in the post deploy command file and deploying our WAR files to a single instance of Payara Micro as previously explained, we can verify we get the appropriate value for each of our applications.

For example, we could send an HTTP POST request to the first service as follows:

```
curl -X POST http://localhost:8080/mpconfigex/webresources/mpconfigexample
```

Then if we inspect the Payara Micro output, we should see the expected value:

```
[2021-09-20T10:05:18.547-0400] [] [INFO] [] [com.ensode.mp.config.example.
MpConfigDemoService] [tid: _ThreadID=79 _ThreadName=http-thread-pool::http-
listener(2)] [timeMillis: 1632146718547] [levelValue: 800] Property value
is: from application source
```

We can then send an HTTP GET request to the second service, which has been deployed in a different WAR file, and verify that the value returned to the client is what we expect.

```
curl  http://localhost:8080/mpappconfigex/webresources/appconfig
Property value is A different value
```

Notice that each service is retrieving the same property name; the values retrieved, though, are different; as expected, they match the values set in the post deploy command file we passed to Payara Micro from the command line.

## Module Configuration Source

Some Jakarta EE applications may have multiple modules; for example, we could deploy one or more WAR files and EJB JAR file inside an Enterprise Archive (EAR) file. The module configuration source allows properties to be visible only for a single module in a multimodule application.

The module configuration source is better suited for Payara Server, as Payara Micro does not support deploying applications in EAR files. If we really want though, we can use the module config source as an alternative to the application configuration source discussed in the previous section.

```
set-config-property --propertyName=my.config.property --propertyValue='from
application source' --source=module --sourceName=mp-config-example-1.0-
SNAPSHOT --moduleName=mp-config-example-1.0-SNAPSHOT
set-config-property --propertyName=my.config.property --propertyValue='A
different value' --source=module --sourceName=mp-application-config-
example-1.0-SNAPSHOT –moduleName=mp-application-config-example-1.0-SNAPSHOT
```

The module configuration source requires sourceName and moduleName parameters; when deploying applications to Payara Micro, the value for both of these parameters must match the application name (i.e., the root name of the WAR file we are deploying).

As with the *application* config source, the *module* config source must be set from a post deployment command file; otherwise, the command will fail as the WAR files won't be deployed yet when the commands are executed; additionally, any properties set on the *module* config source must be retrieved via the appropriate methods in the Config object; injecting the values will result in the applications not deploying properly as the properties are not set until after the application is deployed.

## Cluster Configuration Source

When we start multiple Payara Micro instances on the same network, they automatically form a cluster; this is beneficial as all Payara Micro instances in a cluster can share data. We can set configuration properties at the cluster level by issuing a command in the command file as follows:

```
set-config-property --propertyName=clustered.property.name
--propertyValue='clustered property value' --source=payara
```

We need to use cluster as the source and specify the property name and value as usual.

We can then retrieve the property from any instance of Payara Micro in the cluster as usual, for instance, via injection:

```
@Inject
@ConfigProperty(name = "clustered.property.name")
private String propertyVal;
```

## JDBC Configuration Source

We can use a database table as a MicroProfile configuration source; we set this up via the set-jdbc-config-source asadmin command, specifying the table name, the column containing the property names, and the column containing the property values.

```
create-jdbc-connection-pool --datasourceclassname org.h2.jdbcx.
JdbcDataSource --restype javax.sql.DataSource --property user=sa:password=s
a:url="jdbc:h2:tcp://localhost//tmp/property" PropertyConnectionPool
```

```
create-jdbc-resource --connectionpoolid PropertyConnectionPool
PropertyDataSource
set-jdbc-config-source-configuration --jndiName PropertyDataSource
--tableName PROP_TABLE --keyColumnName PROP_NAME --valueColumnName PROP_VAL
```

Before setting up a JDBC configuration source, we need to have set up a JDBC connection pool and a JDBC resource. In Payara Micro, we can set up a JDBC connection pool via the `create-jdbc-connection-pool` command; we specify an RDBMS specific data source class name via the `--datasourceclassname` argument, the resource type as `javax.sql.DataSource`, and a number of RDBMS specific properties; the last argument is the connection pool id; we need this value when creating a JDBC Resource.

---

In this example, we are using an H2 database; values for `--datasourceclassname` and `--property` will vary depending on the RDBMS we are using (MySQL, Oracle, Sybase, PostgreSQL, etc.); consult your RDBMS documentation for the appropriate values to use.

---

The next step is to create a JDBC resource from the connection pool we just created; we do this via the `create-jdbc-resource` asadmin command, passing the connection pool id of the connection pool we just created. The last argument for `create-jdbc-resource` is the JNDI name of the resource, which we need to create a JDBC configuration source.

Now that we have created a JDBC connection pool and a JDBC resource, we are ready to configure our JDBC config source; we can do this via the `set-jdbc-config-source-configuration` command. In our example, we created a JDBC resource with the JNDI name of `PropertyDataSource`; we pass this value to the `jndiName` argument of the `set-jdbc-config-source-configuration` command. We specify the name of the table containing the properties via the `--tableName` argument and the columns containing the property names and values via `--keyColumnName` and `--valueColumnName`, respectively.

In our example, we are reading properties from a table named `PROP_TABLE`, with property names and values being stored in columns named `PROPERTY_NAME` and `PROPERTY_VAL`, respectively. Figure 5-3 displays our sample table and values.

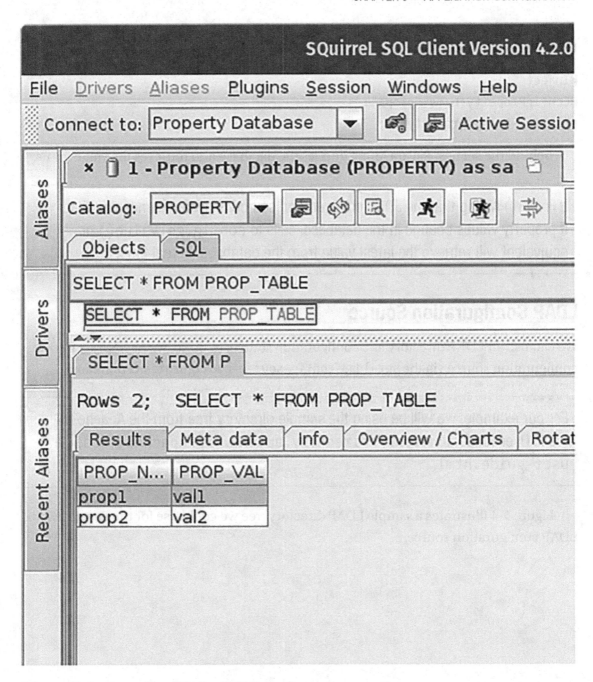

***Figure 5-3.*** *Sample table for JDBC configuration source*

We could retrieve property values via the MicroProfile Config API as usual, for instance, by injecting the configuration value via the @ConfigProperty annotation.

```
@Inject
@ConfigProperty(name="prop1")
private String propertyVal;
```

Behind the scenes, Payara Micro queries the database and retrieves the value for us.

---

It is worth noting that the JDBC configuration source is dynamic, meaning that if property values change in the database, calls to config.getValue() or equivalent will retrieve the latest value from the database, in real time.

---

## LDAP Configuration Source

We can use an LDAP directory as a configuration source; to do so, we need to set the configuration source via the set-ldap-config-source-configuration command.

---

For our example, we will be using the sample directory tree from the Apache DS Basic User Guide at https://directory.apache.org/apacheds/basic-user-guide.html.

---

Figure 5-4 illustrates a sample LDAP directory tree we could use for the Payara Micro LDAP configuration source.

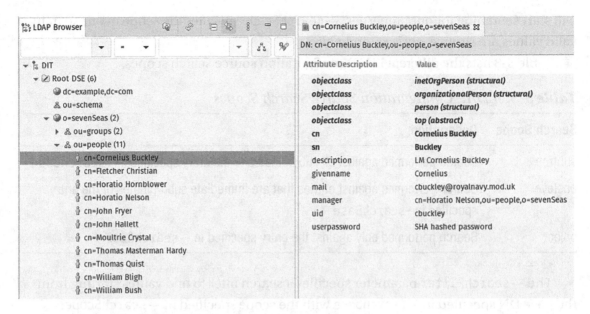

**Figure 5-4.** *Sample LDAP directory tree*

When using LDAP as a configuration source, an entry's attributes serve as property names, with their corresponding values as property values.

In our example, we will retrieve the entry with an sn attribute of *Buckley*; we can then retrieve any attribute for that entry in our code via the MicroProfile Config API.

```
set-ldap-config-source-configuration --enabled=true --dynamic=true
--url=ldap://localhost:10389 --authType=simple --bindDN=uid=admin,ou=system
--bindDNPassword=secret --searchBase=ou=people,o=sevenSeas
--searchScope=subtree --searchFilter=(&(sn=Buckley))
```

We need to enable our configuration source by passing `--enabled=true` as an argument. LDAP configuration sources can either be static or dynamic; if they are static, properties are read once when our application is initially deployed; if the value is updated in the LDAP directory, new values are not read from our application; if we set dynamic to true, then our application will query the LDAP directory in real time, retrieving the latest value in the directory.

We specify the URL of the LDAP server we wish to connect to via the `--url` parameter. Authorization type can either be *none* or *simple*; in our example, we are using simple authentication; we specify the distinguished name (dn) of the user we are connecting to via the `--bindDN` argument and its password via the `--bindDNPassoword`. The `--searchBase` argument specifies the starting node in the LDAP directory where we will start searching for our properties; `--searchScope` specifies the scope of our search; valid values are *subtree, onelevel,* and *object.*

Table 5-3 lists the different LDAP configuration source search scopes.

***Table 5-3.*** *LDAP Configuration Source Search Scopes*

| Search Scope | Description |
|---|---|
| subtree | Search performed against all subordinates of the entry specified in `-searchBase` |
| onelevel | Search performed against entries that are immediate subordinates of the entry specified in `-searchBase` |
| object | Search performed only against the entry specified in `--searchBase` |

The `--searchFilter` parameter specifies a search filter to find values starting from the base DN specified in `--searchBase` with the scope specified in `--searchScope`.

Once we have set up our LDAP configuration source, we can retrieve any attribute from the entry matching our configuration; for example, to retrieve the cn attribute of the LDAP entry in our example, we could invoke `Config.getConfigValue()` as follows:

```
ConfigValue configValue = config.getConfigValue("cn");
```

# Cloud Provider Specific Configuration Sources

Payara Micro can retrieve properties from various cloud provider configuration sources; setting up these properties is beyond the scope of this chapter; retrieving them is no different from what we have already seen. Payara Micro can retrieve properties from the following cloud provider specific configuration sources:

- AWS Secrets

- Azure Secrets

- DynamoDB

- Google Cloud Platform Secrets

- HashiCorp Secrets

Consult your cloud provider documentation for instructions on how to set properties on the preceding configuration sources.

# Custom Configuration Sources

So far, we've discussed all MicroProfile Config standard configuration sources, as well as Payara specific MicroProfile Config configuration sources. If none of the provided configuration sources meet our needs, we can implement our own custom MicroProfile Config configuration source.

To develop a custom MicroProfile Config configuration source, we need to implement the `org.eclipse.microprofile.config.spi.ConfigSource` interface. This interface has three abstract methods:

> `public Set<String> getPropertyNames()` returns a set containing all the property names as strings.

> `public String getValue(String propName)` returns the String value of a property; it expects the property name as an argument.

> `public String getName()` returns the name of our custom configuration source.

At a minimum, we need to implement the preceding three methods in our custom configuration source. Additionally, the `ConfigSource` interface has two default methods, which we could optionally override as well:

`public int getOrdinal()` returns the ordinal value of our custom configuration source; if we don't override this method, then the ordinal value of our configuration source defaults to 100.

`public Map<String, String> getProperties()` returns a map containing keys of our configuration source as keys and the string value of each property as the corresponding value.

The following example illustrates how to implement a custom MicroProfile Config configuration source:

```
package com.ensode.mpcustomconfigsource;

//imports omitted

public class ExternalPropertyFileConfigSource implements
  ConfigSource {

  private static final Logger LOGGER =
    Logger.getLogger(
    ExternalPropertyFileConfigSource.class.getName());
```

```java
private static final String CONFIG_SOURCE_NAME =
  "ExternalPropFile";

private Map propertyMap;

public ExternalPropertyFileConfigSource() throws IOException {
  Properties properties = new Properties();
  String homeDir = System.getProperty("user.home");
  String configFilePath = String.format(
      "%s/config/config.properties", homeDir);
  InputStream inputStream;

  try {
    inputStream = new FileInputStream(configFilePath);
    properties.load(inputStream);
  } catch (FileNotFoundException ex) {
    LOGGER.log(Level.SEVERE, String.format(
        "%s not found!", configFilePath), ex);
  }

  propertyMap = (Map) properties;

}

@Override
public Set<String> getPropertyNames() {
  return propertyMap.keySet();
}

@Override
public String getValue(String propName) {

  String retVal = null;

  var propVal = propertyMap.get(propName);

  if (propVal != null) {
    retVal = propVal.toString();
  }
```

```
    return retVal;
}

@Override
public String getName() {
  return CONFIG_SOURCE_NAME;
}

}
```

In this example, we are reading properties from a property file in a named *config. properties* in a *config* subdirectory in the user's home directory. In the constructor for our class, we read the property file and populate a Map implementation with its property names and keys, with the corresponding values as values.

Our getPropertyNames() implementation simply returns the value of the keySet() method in our map, which does exactly what we need, return the property names in our configuration source in a set.

Our getValue() implementation simply retrieves the value from the map containing our properties and returns its toString() implementation; if the property name does not exist or is null, we simply return null.

We named our custom configuration source *"ExternalPropFile"*; we assigned this value to the CONFIG_SOURCE_NAME constant and returned this constant from our getName() implementation.

Before we can use our custom configuration source, we need to register it; we can do this by creating a file named *org.eclipse.microprofile.config.spi.ConfigSource* containing the fully qualified name of our custom configuration source. In our example, the file would contain the fully qualified name of the example class before, as follows:

```
com.ensode.mpcustomconfigsource.ExternalPropertyFileConfigSource
```

We need to place this file under *META-INF/services* directory in our WAR file. When using Maven to build our code, we can place the file under *src/main/resources/ META-INF/services*; Maven will place it in the correct location when building our code. Figure 5-5 illustrates the correct directory tree.

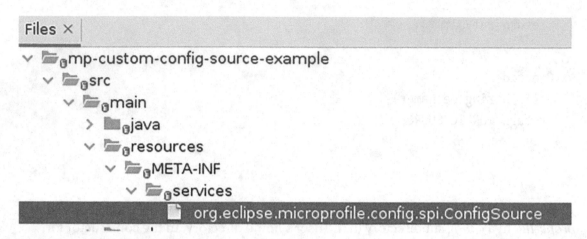

***Figure 5-5.*** *Custom configuration source directory tree*

We can then retrieve properties as usual via the MicroProfile Config API. Suppose our external property file had a couple of properties as follows:

```
sample.property1=first value
sample.property2=second value
```

We could retrieve the value of one of the properties via injection or via the Config class as usual, for instance, injecting the property value as follows:

```
@Inject
@ConfigProperty(name = "sample.property1")
private String prop1;
```

# Dynamic Properties

Dynamic properties allow MicroProfile Config to retrieve up-to-date values for properties in real time. Most standard configuration sources are static, meaning that if the value in the underlying configuration source changes, the MicroProfile Config API won't pick up the change; instead, the value will remain what it was when our application was deployed.

Dynamic properties are properties that will change in real time if the value in the source changes. In most cases, we will have to develop a custom configuration source if we want to implement dynamic properties. The following example is an updated version of the external property file configuration source we discussed in the previous section; this version will update values dynamically.

```java
package com.ensode.mpdynamicconfigsource;

//imports omitted

public class DynamicExternalPropertyFileConfigSource implements
  ConfigSource {

  private static final String CONFIG_SOURCE_NAME =
   "DynamicExternalPropFile";

  private static final Logger LOGGER = Logger.getLogger(
    DynamicExternalPropertyFileConfigSource.class.getName());

  private Map propertyMap;
  String configFileDir;

  public DynamicExternalPropertyFileConfigSource() throws
    IOException, InterruptedException {
    String homeDir = System.getProperty("user.home");
    configFileDir = String.format("%s/config", homeDir);

    updateProperties();
  }

  private void updateProperties() throws IOException {
    Properties properties = new Properties();
    String configFilePath = String.format(
      "%s/config.properties", configFileDir);

    InputStream inputStream;

    try {
      inputStream = new FileInputStream(configFilePath);
      properties.load(inputStream);
    } catch (FileNotFoundException ex) {
      LOGGER.log(Level.SEVERE, String.format(
        "%s not found!", configFilePath), ex);
    }
```

```java
    propertyMap = (Map) properties;
  }

  @Override
  public Set<String> getPropertyNames() {
    return propertyMap.keySet();
  }

  @Override
  public String getValue(String propName) {
    String retVal = null;
    try {
      updateProperties();
      var propVal = propertyMap.get(propName);

      if (propVal != null) {
        retVal = propVal.toString();
      }

    } catch (IOException ex) {
      LOGGER.log(Level.SEVERE, null, ex);
    }

    return retVal;
  }

  @Override
  public String getName() {
    return CONFIG_SOURCE_NAME;
  }

}
```

In this version of our configuration source, we moved the logic to populate the Map containing our properties to the updateProperties() method; we invoke this method both from the constructor and from the getValue() method in our custom configuration source. Since we are repopulating the map every time we read a value, we will always return the latest value stored in the configuration file for any particular property.

Payara Micro may cache read values from the configuration source; it may take up to about a minute for changes in the configuration file to "kick in" and be returned from any calls to the MicroProfile API used to retrieve property values.

# Converters

Values in configuration sources are typically stored as strings; however, sometimes, we need to read a property that isn't a string; it could be a numeric value, for instance, or even a custom object.

## Standard Converters

MicroProfile Config includes converters for all standard Java numeric types, as well as boolean; they work just as you'd expect. For example, a numeric string representing an integer or a float is converted to the appropriate numerical value. For booleans, the following values will resolve to *true*: "true", "yes", "Y", "on", "1"; anything else will resolve to *false*.

The following primitive types and their corresponding object wrappers have standard converters in MicroProfile Config:

- boolean
- int
- long
- float
- double

Additionally, there is also a converter for java.lang.Class that takes a String with the fully qualified name of the class type we wish to initialize; it works like the standard Class.forName() method.

There is also a converter for arrays and lists, in which array elements are separated by commas; for example, the following property, when assigned to an array or list, would result in three separate elements: "a", "b", and "c".

```
my.array.property=a,b,c
```

If we need to include a comma in one of the elements, we can escape it with a backslash.

```
array.property.with.comma=a,b\,c
```

The preceding property would populate an array or list with two elements: "a" and "b,c".

# Payara Micro Specific Converters

In addition to the standard MicroProfile Config converters, Payara Micro includes an additional two converters for java.net.URL and java.net.InetAddress, in which a property containing a valid URL or IP address will be converted to the appropriate type.

# Custom Converters

If we need to convert to a custom type, we can do so by implementing the org.eclipse.microprofile.config.spi.Converter interface. This interface has a single abstract method we need to implement:

```
public T convert(String value)
```

The Converter interface method uses generics so that we can return the appropriate value.

Let's say we had a simple Person class with firstName and lastName properties.

```
package com.ensode.mpconfigcustomconverters;

public class Person {

  private String firstName;
  private String lastName;

  //getters and setters omitted
}
```

Let's write a simple converter that will read the value of a property and convert it to an instance of Person.

```
package com.ensode.mpconfigcustomconverters;

import org.eclipse.microprofile.config.spi.Converter;

public class PersonConverter implements Converter<Person> {

  @Override
  public Person convert(String value) throws
    IllegalArgumentException, NullPointerException {
    Person person = new Person();
    String[] nameArr = value.split(" ");

    person.setFirstName(nameArr[0]);
    person.setLastName(nameArr[1]);

    return person;
  }

}
```

As we can see from the example, to implement a converter, we pass the type we wish to convert to as a generic type parameter; in our example, we wish to convert to an instance of Person; therefore, our type parameter is <Person>. We then implement the body of our convert() method, which will now return an instance of the class we are converting to. In our (admittedly overly simple) example, we simply read a String value, split it using spaces as a delimiter, and assign the first and second elements of the split string to the firstName and lastName properties of the Person class, respectively.

Before we can use our custom converter, we need to register it; we accomplish this by creating a file named org.eclipse.microprofile.config.spi.Converter under the *META-INF/services* directory of our WAR file and placing the fully qualified name of our custom converted in the file. As usual, Maven will place the file in the correct directory in the WAR file if we place it under src/main/resources/META-INF/services in our source code project, as illustrated in Figure 5-6.

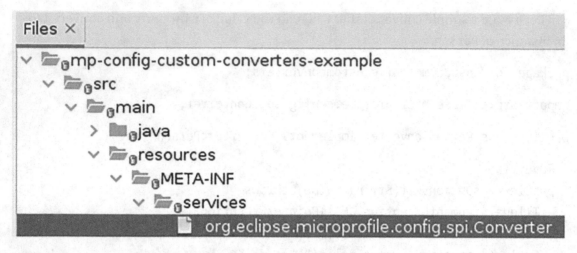

*Figure 5-6.* *Custom converter registration directory tree*

In our example, the contents of the file would look like this:

```
com.ensode.mpconfigcustomconverters.PersonConverter
```

Suppose we had a couple of properties in microprofile-config.properties as follows:

```
customer1=David Heffelfinger
customer2=John Doe
```

Reading either one of these properties and assigning them to an object of type Person would trigger our custom converter.

```
package com.ensode.mpconfigcustomconverters;

//imports omitted

@RequestScoped
@Path("customconverter")
public class CustomConverterService {

  @Inject
  @ConfigProperty(name = "customer1")
  private Person person;
```

```
@GET
@Produces(MediaType.APPLICATION_JSON)
public Person getCustomer() {
  return person;
}

}
```

The preceding RESTful web service would read the value of the customer1 property; our custom converter kicks in since the value is assigned to a variable of type Person. The getCustomer() method would return a JSON representation of the populated Person object when our service receives an HTTP GET request; for example, sending a request with curl

*curl http://localhost:8080/mpconfigcustomconverter/webresources/ customconverter*

would return the following JSON string:

*{"firstName":"David", "lastName":"Heffelfinger"}*

# Summary

In this chapter, we covered how to configure our applications using the MicroProfile Config API.

We discussed standard configuration sources required by the MicroProfile Config specification. Additionally, we covered additional MicroProfile Config configuration sources implemented by Payara Micro. We also saw how to implement our own custom configuration sources.

We also covered how to convert string properties to Java objects via converters. We discussed standard converters provided by the MicroProfile specification, as well as additional converters provided by Payara Micro. Additionally, we saw how to implement our own custom MicroProfile Config converters.

# CHAPTER 6

# Metrics

The MicroProfile Metrics API allows us to easily generate monitoring data (things like CPU load, disk space usage, number of HTTP requests, etc.). Payara Micro provides a metrics endpoint that can provide this data with no additional effort on our part.

There are four MicroProfile metrics endpoints:

- */metrics/base* is defined by the MicroProfile standard, meaning that all MicroProfile implementations (such as Payara Micro) must implement it. It provides information about the JVM that is running our instance of Payara Micro, things like the number of Java classes loaded into memory, JVM uptime, JVM memory information, etc.

- */metrics/vendor* allows us to retrieve vendor-specific metric information.

- */metrics/application* allows us to retrieve our application-specific metrics, which we can generate via annotations.

- */metrics* displays all metric information, including the data in */metrics/base*, */metrics/vendor*, and *metrics/application*.

Data generated by the MicroProfile Metrics API is meant to be read by monitoring tools that can automatically alert us if an application is using too much CPU, memory, disk space, or any other number of warnings. By default, the output of the MicroProfile Config endpoints is in *Prometheus* format.

Prometheus is a very popular open source monitoring tool. Since Prometheus is so popular, the format it uses to read metrics data has been adopted by several other monitoring tools. By generating data in Prometheus format, MicroProfile Config is automatically compatible with several monitoring tools. If we wish to receive metric data in JSON format instead, all we need to do is set the *Accept* HTTP header in our request to *application/json*.

© David R. Heffelfinger 2022
D. R. Heffelfinger, *Payara Micro Revealed*, https://doi.org/10.1007/978-1-4842-8161-1_6

# Base Metrics

We can access base metrics by sending a GET request to the *metrics/base* endpoint of our Payara Micro instance.

For example, using curl to send a request to an instance of Payara Micro running on our local workstation

```
curl http://localhost:8080/metrics/base
```

would result in output similar to the following:

```
# TYPE base_classloader_loadedClasses_count gauge
# HELP base_classloader_loadedClasses_count Displays the number of classes
that are currently loaded in the JVM.
base_classloader_loadedClasses_count 16396
# TYPE base_classloader_loadedClasses_total_total counter
# HELP base_classloader_loadedClasses_total_total Displays the total number
of classes that have been loaded since the JVM has started execution.
base_classloader_loadedClasses_total_total 16396
# TYPE base_classloader_unloadedClasses_total_total counter
# HELP base_classloader_unloadedClasses_total_total Displays the total
number of classes unloaded since the JVM has started execution.
base_classloader_unloadedClasses_total_total 0
# TYPE base_cpu_availableProcessors gauge
# HELP base_cpu_availableProcessors Displays the number of processors
available to the JVM. This value may change during a particular invocation
of the virtual machine.
base_cpu_availableProcessors 8
# TYPE base_cpu_systemLoadAverage gauge
# HELP base_cpu_systemLoadAverage Displays the system load average for the
last minute. The system load average is the sum of the number of runnable
entities queued to the available processors and the number of runnable
entities running on the available processors averaged over a period of
time. The way in which the load average is calculated is operating system
specific but is typically a damped time-dependent average. If the load
average is not available, a negative value is displayed. This attribute
is designed to provide a hint about the system load and may be queried
```

frequently. The load average may be unavailable on some platform where it is expensive to implement this method.

base_cpu_systemLoadAverage 0.32

# TYPE base_gc_time_total counter

# HELP base_gc_time_total Displays the approximate accumulated collection elapsed time in milliseconds. This attribute displays -1 if the collection elapsed time is undefined for this collector. The JVM implementation may use a high resolution timer to measure the elapsed time. This attribute may display the same value even if the collection count has been incremented if the collection elapsed time is very short.

base_gc_time_total{name="G1 Young Generation"} 226

base_gc_time_total{name="G1 Old Generation"} 0

# TYPE base_gc_total_total counter

# HELP base_gc_total_total Displays the total number of collections that have occurred. This attribute lists -1 if the collection count is undefined for this collector.

base_gc_total_total{name="G1 Young Generation"} 15

base_gc_total_total{name="G1 Old Generation"} 0

# TYPE base_jvm_uptime_seconds gauge

# HELP base_jvm_uptime_seconds Displays the uptime of the JVM in milliseconds.

base_jvm_uptime_seconds 4745.731

# TYPE base_memory_committedHeap_bytes gauge

# HELP base_memory_committedHeap_bytes Displays the amount of memory in bytes that is committed for the JVM to use.

base_memory_committedHeap_bytes 8.09500672E8

# TYPE base_memory_committedNonHeap_bytes gauge

# HELP base_memory_committedNonHeap_bytes Displays the amount of memory in bytes that is committed for the JVM to use.

base_memory_committedNonHeap_bytes 1.3787136E8

# TYPE base_memory_maxHeap_bytes gauge

# HELP base_memory_maxHeap_bytes Displays the maximum amount of memory in bytes that can be used for HeapMemory.

base_memory_maxHeap_bytes 1.0479468544E10

# TYPE base_memory_maxNonHeap_bytes gauge

```
# HELP base_memory_maxNonHeap_bytes Displays the maximum amount of memory
in bytes that can be used for NonHeapMemory.
base_memory_maxNonHeap_bytes -1
# TYPE base_memory_usedHeap_bytes gauge
# HELP base_memory_usedHeap_bytes Displays the amount of used memory
in bytes.
base_memory_usedHeap_bytes 3.10751824E8
# TYPE base_memory_usedNonHeap_bytes gauge
# HELP base_memory_usedNonHeap_bytes Displays the amount of used memory
in bytes.
base_memory_usedNonHeap_bytes 1.31463504E8
# TYPE base_thread_count gauge
# HELP base_thread_count Displays the current number of live threads
including both daemon and non-daemon threads.
base_thread_count 75
# TYPE base_thread_daemon_count gauge
# HELP base_thread_daemon_count Displays the current number of live daemon
threads.
base_thread_daemon_count 62
# TYPE base_thread_max_count gauge
# HELP base_thread_max_count Displays the peak live thread count since the
Java virtual machine started or peak was reset. This includes daemon and
non-daemon threads.
base_thread_max_count 100
```

The preceding output is in the default Prometheus format; if we wish to receive the data in JSON format, we need to set the *Accept* request header to *application/json*; for instance, using curl

```
curl -H "Accept: application/json"  http://localhost:8080/metrics/base
```

would return output in JSON format.

```
{
    "classloader.loadedClasses.count": 16398.0,
    "classloader.loadedClasses.total": 16398,
    "classloader.unloadedClasses.total": 0,
    "cpu.availableProcessors": 8.0,
```

```
    "cpu.systemLoadAverage": 0.29,
    "gc.time;name=G1 Young Generation": 226,
    "gc.time;name=G1 Old Generation": 0,
    "gc.total;name=G1 Young Generation": 15,
    "gc.total;name=G1 Old Generation": 0,
    "jvm.uptime": 5249144.0,
    "memory.committedHeap": 809500672,
    "memory.committedNonHeap": 138002432,
    "memory.maxHeap": 10479468544,
    "memory.maxNonHeap": -1.0,
    "memory.usedHeap": 3.904436E+8,
    "memory.usedNonHeap": 131634184,
    "thread.count": 75.0,
    "thread.daemon.count": 62.0,
    "thread.max.count": 100.0
}
```

# Vendor Metrics

At the time of writing, Payara Micro provides a single vendor metric; we can access it by sending an HTTP request to /metrics/vendor:

```
curl http://localhost:8080/metrics/vendor
```

which would result in output similar to the following:

```
# TYPE vendor_system_cpu_load gauge
# HELP vendor_system_cpu_load Display the "recent cpu usage" for the whole
system. This value is a double in the [0.0,1.0] interval. A value of 0.0
means that all CPUs were idle during the recent period of time observed,
while a value of 1.0 means that all CPUs were actively running 100% of
the time during the recent period being observed. All values betweens 0.0
and 1.0 are possible depending of the activities going on in the system.
If the system recent cpu usage is not available, the method returns a
negative value.
vendor_system_cpu_load 0.021788129226145758
```

Or if we wish to receive Payara Micro's vendor-specific metric data in JSON format, we set the *Accept* HTTP header as usual:

```
curl -H "Accept: application/json"  http://localhost:8080/metrics/vendor
```

which would, unsurprisingly, result in getting the Payara Micro vendor-specific metric data in JSON format.

```
{
    "system.cpu.load": 0.015595463137996219
}
```

---

Payara Server allows us to expose JMX beans as custom vendor metrics; at the time of writing, this functionality is not available in Payara Micro.

---

# Application Metrics

MicroProfile metrics provides a number of annotations we can use to annotate our methods, which can provide application metrics with very little effort on our part.

Most MicroProfile metrics annotations have a common set of attributes:

- absolute: A boolean value indicating if the name of the metric should be absolute or if it should be appended to the fully qualified name of the class.

- description: A description for our metric.

- displayName: A human-readable display for the metric.

- name: The name of the metric, if not specified, defaults to the method name we are annotating.

- tags: Used to differentiate metrics with the same name.

- unit: The unit of measurement for the metric.

# @Counted

The @Counted annotation indicates the number of times our method has been called; the counter value is increased automatically every time our method gets called.

```
@GET
@Counted
@Path("counted")
@Produces(MediaType.TEXT_PLAIN)
public String countedExample() {
    return "Counter was just increased\n";
}
```

After calling our endpoint a few times, we can see the output by sending a GET request to the /metrics/application endpoint in Payara Micro:

```
# TYPE application_com_ensode_applicationmetrics_MetricsDemo_
countedExample_total counter
application_com_ensode_applicationmetrics_MetricsDemo_countedExample_
total{_app="application-metrics-1.0-snapshot"} 3
```

Or in JSON format:

```
{
    "com.ensode.applicationmetrics.MetricsDemo.countedExample;_
    app=application-metrics-1.0-snapshot": 3
}
```

# @Gauge

This annotation can only be applied to methods returning numeric objects (Long, Short, Integer, Float, Double) or their corresponding primitive types; it exposes the return value as a metric.@GET

```
@Gauge(unit = "some unit")
@Path("gauge")
@Produces(MediaType.TEXT_PLAIN)
```

```
public int gaugeExample() {
  gaugeVal += 2;
  return gaugeVal;
}
```

The unit attribute of @Gauge is required; we can assign any arbitrary string value to it; for instance, if we were returning the number of employees in an organization, the unit could be "employees"; if we were returning the number of widgets produced in a factory, the unit could be "widgets"; and so on and so forth.

Output for @Gauge in Prometheus format looks like the following:

```
# TYPE application_com_ensode_applicationmetrics_MetricsDemo_gaugeExample_
some_unit gauge
application_com_ensode_applicationmetrics_MetricsDemo_gaugeExample_some_
unit{_app="application-metrics-1.0-snapshot"} 8
```

Or in JSON format:

```
"com.ensode.applicationmetrics.MetricsDemo.gaugeExample;_app=application-
metrics-1.0-snapshot": 10
{
  "com.ensode.applicationmetrics.MetricsDemo.gaugeExample;_app=application-
  metrics-1.0-snapshot": 8
}
```

# @ConcurrentGauge

This annotation displays the number of concurrent calls to a method (typically a REST endpoint) at any particular point in time.

```
@GET
@ConcurrentGauge
@Path("concurrentGauge")
@Produces(MediaType.TEXT_PLAIN)
public void concurrentGaugeExample() throws InterruptedException {
  TimeUnit.SECONDS.sleep(10);
}
```

In our example, we are simply sleeping for ten seconds; this allows us to make a few calls to the endpoint and call the metrics endpoint so that we can get relevant example data.

Output for @ConcurrentGauge looks like the following:

```
# TYPE application_com_ensode_applicationmetrics_MetricsDemo_
concurrentGaugeExample_current gauge
application_com_ensode_applicationmetrics_MetricsDemo_
concurrentGaugeExample_current{_app="application-metrics-1.0-snapshot"} 3
# TYPE application_com_ensode_applicationmetrics_MetricsDemo_
concurrentGaugeExample_min gauge
application_com_ensode_applicationmetrics_MetricsDemo_
concurrentGaugeExample_min{_app="application-metrics-1.0-snapshot"} 0
# TYPE application_com_ensode_applicationmetrics_MetricsDemo_
concurrentGaugeExample_max gauge
application_com_ensode_applicationmetrics_MetricsDemo_
concurrentGaugeExample_max{_app="application-metrics-1.0-snapshot"} 3
```

@ConcurrentGauge returns not only the concurrent number of invocations to the method but also the minimum and maximum number of concurrent invocations to the method in the previous minute.

JSON format output of @ConcurrentGauge looks as follows:

```
{
  "com.ensode.applicationmetrics.MetricsDemo.concurrentGaugeExample": {
      "current;_app=application-metrics-1.0-snapshot": 3,
      "min;_app=application-metrics-1.0-snapshot": 0,
      "max;_app=application-metrics-1.0-snapshot": 3
  }
}
```

## @Metered

This annotation generates the number of times a method has been called, as well as the rate per second of calls during the lifetime of the application, as well as the rate per second in the last minute, last five minutes, and last fifteen minutes.

```
@GET
@Metered
@Path("metered")
@Produces(MediaType.TEXT_PLAIN)
public String meteredExample() {
  return "Metered method invoked\n";
}
```

Output of @Metered looks like the following:

```
application_com_ensode_applicationmetrics_MetricsDemo_meteredExample_
total{_app="application-metrics-1.0-snapshot"} 5
18k
# TYPE application_com_ensode_applicationmetrics_MetricsDemo_
meteredExample_rate_per_second gauge
application_com_ensode_applicationmetrics_MetricsDemo_meteredExample_rate_
per_second{_app="application-metrics-1.0-snapshot"} 0.0072698202140590275
# TYPE application_com_ensode_applicationmetrics_MetricsDemo_
meteredExample_one_min_rate_per_second gauge
application_com_ensode_applicationmetrics_MetricsDemo_meteredExample_
one_min_rate_per_second{_app="application-metrics-1.0-snapshot"}
0.01806938732711853
# TYPE application_com_ensode_applicationmetrics_MetricsDemo_
meteredExample_five_min_rate_per_second gauge
application_com_ensode_applicationmetrics_MetricsDemo_meteredExample_
five_min_rate_per_second{_app="application-metrics-1.0-snapshot"}
0.012251339396869875
# TYPE application_com_ensode_applicationmetrics_MetricsDemo_
meteredExample_fifteen_min_rate_per_second gauge
application_com_ensode_applicationmetrics_MetricsDemo_meteredExample_
fifteen_min_rate_per_second{_app="application-metrics-1.0-snapshot"}
0.005013244558508323
```

Equivalent JSON format:

```
{
  "com.ensode.applicationmetrics.MetricsDemo.meteredExample": {
      "count;_app=application-metrics-1.0-snapshot": 5,
```

```
    "meanRate;_app=application-metrics-1.0-snapshot":
    0.0060812930956421875,
    "oneMinRate;_app=application-metrics-1.0-snapshot":
    0.0019044994125862731,
    "fiveMinRate;_app=application-metrics-1.0-snapshot":
    0.007811798894517148,
    "fifteenMinRate;_app=application-metrics-1.0-snapshot":
    0.004314939579277629
  }
}
```

# @Timed

This annotation generates statistics (mean, standard deviation, etc.) about the time it takes to finish a method invocation.

```
@GET
@Timed
@Path("timed")
@Produces(MediaType.TEXT_PLAIN)
public void timedExample() throws InterruptedException {
  TimeUnit.SECONDS.sleep(2);
}
```

Output of @Timed looks like the following:

```
# TYPE application_com_ensode_applicationmetrics_MetricsDemo_timedExample_
rate_per_second gauge
application_com_ensode_applicationmetrics_MetricsDemo_timedExample_rate_
per_second{_app="application-metrics-1.0-snapshot"} 0.1465568677874658
# TYPE application_com_ensode_applicationmetrics_MetricsDemo_timedExample_
one_min_rate_per_second gauge
application_com_ensode_applicationmetrics_MetricsDemo_timedExample_one_min_
rate_per_second{_app="application-metrics-1.0-snapshot"} 0.2
# TYPE application_com_ensode_applicationmetrics_MetricsDemo_timedExample_
five_min_rate_per_second gauge
```

```
application_com_ensode_applicationmetrics_MetricsDemo_timedExample_five_
min_rate_per_second{_app="application-metrics-1.0-snapshot"} 0.2
# TYPE application_com_ensode_applicationmetrics_MetricsDemo_timedExample_
fifteen_min_rate_per_second gauge
application_com_ensode_applicationmetrics_MetricsDemo_timedExample_fifteen_
min_rate_per_second{_app="application-metrics-1.0-snapshot"} 0.2
# TYPE application_com_ensode_applicationmetrics_MetricsDemo_timedExample_
mean_seconds gauge
application_com_ensode_applicationmetrics_MetricsDemo_timedExample_mean_
seconds{_app="application-metrics-1.0-snapshot"} 2.000146096
# TYPE application_com_ensode_applicationmetrics_MetricsDemo_timedExample_
max_seconds gauge
application_com_ensode_applicationmetrics_MetricsDemo_timedExample_max_
seconds{_app="application-metrics-1.0-snapshot"} 2.000146096
# TYPE application_com_ensode_applicationmetrics_MetricsDemo_timedExample_
min_seconds gauge
application_com_ensode_applicationmetrics_MetricsDemo_timedExample_min_
seconds{_app="application-metrics-1.0-snapshot"} 2.000146096
# TYPE application_com_ensode_applicationmetrics_MetricsDemo_timedExample_
stddev_seconds gauge
application_com_ensode_applicationmetrics_MetricsDemo_timedExample_stddev_
seconds{_app="application-metrics-1.0-snapshot"} 0
# TYPE application_com_ensode_applicationmetrics_MetricsDemo_timedExample_
seconds summary
application_com_ensode_applicationmetrics_MetricsDemo_timedExample_seconds_
count{_app="application-metrics-1.0-snapshot"} 1
application_com_ensode_applicationmetrics_MetricsDemo_timedExample_seconds_
sum{_app="application-metrics-1.0-snapshot"} 2.000146096
application_com_ensode_applicationmetrics_MetricsDemo_timedExample_
seconds{_app="application-metrics-1.0-snapshot",quantile="0.5"} 2.000146096
application_com_ensode_applicationmetrics_MetricsDemo_timedExample_
seconds{_app="application-metrics-1.0-snapshot",quantile="0.75"}
2.000146096
application_com_ensode_applicationmetrics_MetricsDemo_timedExample_
seconds{_app="application-metrics-1.0-snapshot",quantile="0.95"}
2.000146096
```

```
application_com_ensode_applicationmetrics_MetricsDemo_timedExample_
seconds{_app="application-metrics-1.0-snapshot",quantile="0.98"}
2.000146096
application_com_ensode_applicationmetrics_MetricsDemo_timedExample_
seconds{_app="application-metrics-1.0-snapshot",quantile="0.99"}
2.000146096
application_com_ensode_applicationmetrics_MetricsDemo_timedExample_
seconds{_app="application-metrics-1.0-snapshot",quantile="0.999"}
2.000146096
```

Output of @Timed in JSON format looks like the following:

```
{
  "com.ensode.applicationmetrics.MetricsDemo.timedExample": {
      "elapsedTime;_app=application-metrics-1.0-snapshot": 2000,
      "count;_app=application-metrics-1.0-snapshot": 1,
      "meanRate;_app=application-metrics-1.0-snapshot":
      0.005027283318233858,
      "oneMinRate;_app=application-metrics-1.0-snapshot":
      0.008428768701855296,
      "fiveMinRate;_app=application-metrics-1.0-snapshot":
      0.10616389011240278,
      "fifteenMinRate;_app=application-metrics-1.0-snapshot":
      0.16193681939667523,
      "min;_app=application-metrics-1.0-snapshot": 2000146096,
      "max;_app=application-metrics-1.0-snapshot": 2000146096,
      "mean;_app=application-metrics-1.0-snapshot": 2000146096,
      "stddev;_app=application-metrics-1.0-snapshot": 0.0,
      "p50;_app=application-metrics-1.0-snapshot": 2000146096,
      "p75;_app=application-metrics-1.0-snapshot": 2000146096,
      "p95;_app=application-metrics-1.0-snapshot": 2000146096,
      "p98;_app=application-metrics-1.0-snapshot": 2000146096,
      "p99;_app=application-metrics-1.0-snapshot": 2000146096,
      "p999;_app=application-metrics-1.0-snapshot": 2000146096
}
```

# @SimplyTimed

Sometimes, we don't need all the data that @Timed provides; @SimplyTimed provides only a few pieces of data, namely, the elapsed time across all invocations, the number of times the method has been invoked, and the maximum and minimum times the method has taken to execute.

```
@GET
@SimplyTimed
@Path("simplytimed")
@Produces(MediaType.TEXT_PLAIN)
public void simplyTimedExample() throws InterruptedException {
  TimeUnit.SECONDS.sleep(3);
}
```

Output of @SimplyTimed looks like the following:

```
# TYPE application_com_ensode_applicationmetrics_MetricsDemo_
simplyTimedExample_elapsedTime_seconds gauge
application_com_ensode_applicationmetrics_MetricsDemo_simplyTimedExample_
elapsedTime_seconds{_app="application-metrics-1.0-snapshot"} 18.001398226
# TYPE application_com_ensode_applicationmetrics_MetricsDemo_
simplyTimedExample_maxTimeDuration_seconds gauge
application_com_ensode_applicationmetrics_MetricsDemo_simplyTimedExample_
maxTimeDuration_seconds{_app="application-metrics-1.0-snapshot"} 3.000302743
# TYPE application_com_ensode_applicationmetrics_MetricsDemo_
simplyTimedExample_minTimeDuration_seconds gauge
100 11184    0 11184    0    0  1365k      0 --:--:-- --:--:-- --:--:-- 1365k
application_com_ensode_applicationmetrics_MetricsDemo_simplyTimedExample_
minTimeDuration_seconds{_app="application-metrics-1.0-snapshot"} 3.000122495
```

Or in JSON format:

```
{
  "com.ensode.applicationmetrics.MetricsDemo.simplyTimedExample": {
      "count;_app=application-metrics-1.0-snapshot": 11,
      "elapsedTime;_app=application-metrics-1.0-snapshot": 33002,
```

```
    "maxTimeDuration;_app=application-metrics-1.0-snapshot": 3000,
    "minTimeDuration;_app=application-metrics-1.0-snapshot": 3000
  }
}
```

# Programmatic Application Metrics

Most MicroProfile metrics annotations have an equivalent implementation we can use programmatically. For example, the Counter interface is the equivalent of the @Counted annotation. Implementing metrics programmatically allows us to exert more control over the value of our annotations; with Counter, for example, we can increase or even decrease the counter based on our business requirements, as opposed to the @Counted annotation, which only increases the counter when the annotated method is invoked, and there is no way to decrease the counter via the annotation.

The following example illustrates the usage of the MicroProfile metrics Counted interface.

```
package com.ensode.application.metrics.programmatic;

//imports omitted

@ApplicationScoped
@Path("employeeservice")
public class EmployeeResource {

  @Inject
  @Metric
  private Counter employeeCounter;

  private List<Employee> employeeList =
    snew CopyOnWriteArrayList<>(); //thread safe

  @PUT
  @Consumes(MediaType.APPLICATION_JSON)
  public void hireEmployee(Employee employee) {
    employeeList.add(employee);
    employeeCounter.inc();
  }
```

```
@DELETE
@Consumes(MediaType.APPLICATION_JSON)
public void fireEmployee(@QueryParam("firstName") String firstName,
@QueryParam("lastName") String lastName) {

  Optional<Employee> employeeToFire =
    employeeList.stream().filter(emp →
      emp.getFirstName().equals(firstName) &&
      emp.getLastName().equals(lastName)).findAny();
  employeeToFire.ifPresent(
        emp -> {
          employeeList.remove(emp);
          employeeCounter.inc(-1);
        });
  }
}
```

In the preceding example, we inject an implementation of the Counter interface via the CDI @Inject annotation and the MicroProfile @Metric annotation. @Metric identifies the counter instance as a metric and lets the MicroProfile Metrics API know it needs to use it to generate application-specific metrics.

Once we have injected a Counter implementation, we can increase or decrease the counter as our business requirements dictate. In our example, the counter is keeping track of the number of employees in a List; it increases every time an employee is hired and decreases every time an employee is fired.

Table 6-1 lists metrics we can use programmatically, along with their annotation equivalents.

***Table 6-1.*** *Programmatic Metrics*

| Metric Interface | Annotation |
| --- | --- |
| Counter | @Counted |
| ConcurrentGauge | @ConcurrentGauge |
| SimpleTimer | @SimpleTimer |
| Timer | @Timer |

We already saw an example of the Counter interface; `ConcurrentGauge` works similarly, but it provides a `dec()` method we can use to decrement the counter. `Timer` and `SimpleTimer` both provide overloaded methods of a `time()` method; taking an instance of a `Callable` or `Runnable` interface implementation (typically implemented as a lambda expression), we can use to time-specific events in our application. For example, if we wanted to find out how long it takes to add an employee to the Employee list, we could do it as follows:

```
package com.ensode.application.metrics.programmatic;

//imports omitted

@ApplicationScoped
@Path("employeeservice")
public class EmployeeResource {

  @Inject
  @Metric
  private SimpleTimer employeeAddSimpleTimer;

  private List<Employee> employeeList = new CopyOnWriteArrayList<>(); //
  thread safe

  @PUT
  @Consumes(MediaType.APPLICATION_JSON)
  public void hireEmployee(Employee employee) {
    employeeAddSimpleTimer.time(() -> {
      employeeList.add(employee);
    });
  }
}
```

In this example, we inject an instance of `SimpleTimer` via the `@Inject` and `@Metric` annotations as usual, when we wrap the call to add an employee to the list in a lambda expression and pass the resulting `Runnable` implementation to the `time()` method in our `SimpleTimer`.

There is one more metric provided by the MicroProfile API called a `Histogram`, which calculates the distribution of a value. To use Histogram, we inject it as usual and then invoke its `update()` method to add values to the histogram, as illustrated in the following example.

117

```
package com.ensode.application.metrics.programmatic;

//imports omitted

@ApplicationScoped
@Path("employeeservice")
public class EmployeeResource {

  @Inject
  @Metric
  private Histogram histogram;

  private List<Employee> employeeList = new CopyOnWriteArrayList<>();
  //thread safe

  @PUT
  @Consumes(MediaType.APPLICATION_JSON)
  public void hireEmployee(Employee employee) {

    employeeList.add(employee);
    histogram.update(employeeList.size());
  }
}
```

# Configuring MicroProfile Metrics in Payara Micro

We can configure metrics in Payara Micro via the set-metrics-configuration asadmin command via a command file passed as a post boot command file or similar.

## Disabling Metrics

Payara Micro enables metrics by default; if we wish to disable them, we can use the following asadmin command:

```
set-metrics-configuration --enabled=false
```

## Securing Metrics

By default, the */metrics* endpoint is unsecured, meaning any random unauthenticated user can access it.

If we wish to secure it, we can do so by issuing the following asadmin command:

```
set-metrics-configuation --securityenabled=true
```

When securing the */metrics* endpoint, we can specify which roles have access to it as follows:

```
set-metrics-configuration --roles=role1,role2,role3
```

The value of the --roles argument is a comma-separated list of roles allowed to access the generated metrics.

## Customizing the Metrics Endpoint

By default, metrics can be retrieved via the /metrics endpoint. We can use a different endpoint if we wish.

```
set-metrics-configuration --endpoint=foo
```

The value of the --endpoint argument is the context root of our custom metrics endpoint.

## Static Metrics

By default, metrics are updated dynamically as our application runs; if, instead, we wish to have static metrics that won't update until our application restarts, we can do so as follows:

```
set-metrics-configuration --dynamic=false
```

# Summary

In this chapter, we covered Payara Micro support for the MicroProfile Metrics API. We generate metrics to be consumed by monitoring tools. We covered how to use annotations provided by MicroProfile metrics to generate metrics with almost no effort on our part; we also saw how we can generate metrics programmatically for cases when we need more control on how to generate those metrics.

# CHAPTER 7

# High Availability and Fault Tolerance

When developing an application using a microservices architecture, we typically have a number of services that depend on one another. It is possible that one or more of the services may go down, possibly bringing the whole system down with them. The MicroProfile Fault Tolerance API provides functionality we can use to mitigate this risk, providing several annotations we can use to configure how the system behaves when one or more microservices are not available or otherwise not working properly.

## Asynchronously Calling RESTful Web Service Endpoints

MicroProfile Fault Tolerance provides the @Asynchronous annotation, which allows RESTful web service endpoints to be invoked asynchronously. This allows the client to continue processing and not block when invoking a service that may take a long time. This is especially useful when the client has to call multiple services that may each take a while to return; by invoking them asynchronously, these services can execute in parallel, reducing the time the client would have to wait to get the results.

The @Asynchronous annotation can be applied to methods in request scoped CDI beans; the method must return an implementation of either Future or CompletionStage interfaces. A return type of CompletionStage is preferred as in this case any other fault tolerance annotations applied to the method will still be applied if the invoked method throws an exception; this is not the case with methods returning Future.

---

Recall that we can turn any RESTful web service into a CDI bean simply by applying one of the scope annotations, such as @RequestScoped.

---

© David R. Heffelfinger 2022
D. R. Heffelfinger, *Payara Micro Revealed*, https://doi.org/10.1007/978-1-4842-8161-1_7

The following example illustrates how we can indicate that our endpoint may be called asynchronously:

```
package com.ensode.faulttolerance;

//imports omitted

@RequestScoped
@Path("faulttoleranceexample")
public class FaulToleranceExampleResource {

  @Asynchronous
  @GET
  @Path("async")
  @Produces(MediaType.TEXT_PLAIN)
  public CompletionStage<Integer> getAsynchronousValue()
    throws InterruptedException {
    TimeUnit.SECONDS.sleep(5);
    return CompletableFuture.completedStage(18);
  }

  @Asynchronous
  @GET
  @Path("async2")
  @Produces(MediaType.TEXT_PLAIN)
  public CompletionStage<Integer> getAnotherAsynchronousValue()
    throws InterruptedException {
    TimeUnit.SECONDS.sleep(7);
    return CompletableFuture.completedStage(24);
  }

}
```

As we can see in the example, all we have to do is annotate any methods to be invoked asynchronously with @Asynchronous and make sure the method returns either a Future or a CompletionStage; when a client invokes our asynchronous methods, control goes back immediately to the client; the client won't block waiting for a result.

When using the MicroProfile REST client API to develop our client, we apply the @Asynchronous annotations used on the service to our rest client interface methods.

```
package com.ensode.fault.toleranceclient;

//imports omitted

@RegisterRestClient
@Path("faulttoleranceexample")
public interface FaultToleranceExampleResourceClient {

  @Asynchronous
  @GET
  @Path("async")
  @Produces(MediaType.TEXT_PLAIN)
  public CompletionStage<Integer> getAsynchronousValue()
    throws InterruptedException;

  @Asynchronous
  @GET
  @Path("async2")
  @Produces(MediaType.TEXT_PLAIN)
  public CompletionStage<Integer> getAnotherAsynchronousValue()
    throws InterruptedException;
}
```

Then the service acting as a client for the asynchronous methods would use our client interface as usual.

```
package com.ensode.fault.toleranceclient;

//imports omitted

@Path("/faulttoleranceclient")
public class FaultToleranceClientService {

  @Inject
  @RestClient
  private FaultToleranceExampleResourceClient client;

  @GET
  @Produces(MediaType.TEXT_PLAIN)
  public String get() throws InterruptedException,
```

```
ExecutionException {
Integer answer;
Integer value1;
Integer value2;
String retVal;

CompletionStage<Integer> asynchronousValue =
  client.getAsynchronousValue();

CompletionStage<Integer> asynchronousValue2 =
  client.getAnotherAsynchronousValue();

value1 = asynchronousValue.toCompletableFuture().get();
value2 = asynchronousValue2.toCompletableFuture().get();

answer = value1 + value2;
retVal = String.format("The answer is %d\n", answer);

return retVal;
  }

}
```

One of the invoked methods takes approximately five seconds to return a value; the other one takes approximately seven seconds. Had we called this method synchronously, the client would have had to wait approximately 12 seconds to obtain both results; since we are calling them asynchronously (they run in parallel), the client only has to block for approximately seven seconds to obtain both results.

## Limit Concurrent Execution to Avoid Overloading the System

MicroProfile Fault Tolerance provides the @Bulkhead annotation, named after the Bulkhead design pattern, since it allows us to implement this pattern with minimal effort. @Bulkhead can be used to specify the maximum number of concurrent instances for a RESTful web service endpoint.

There are two ways to use the @Bulkhead annotation: the semaphore style and the thread pool style.

# Using Semaphores for Synchronous Endpoints

When using the semaphore style, the value argument of the annotation indicates the maximum number of concurrent invocations to a microservice endpoint; any additional attempts for concurrent invocations result in a BulkheadException.

The following example illustrates the semaphore style usage of the @Bulkhead annotation:

```
package com.ensode.faulttolerance;

//imports omitted

@RequestScoped
@Path("faulttoleranceexample")
public class FaulToleranceExampleResource {

  @Inject
  private ConcurrentInvocationCounter concurrentInvocationCounter;

  @POST
  @Path("semaphorebulkhead")
  @Bulkhead(3)
  @Produces(MediaType.TEXT_PLAIN)
  public String semaphoreBulkHeadDemo() throws
    InterruptedException {

    String retVal;
    concurrentInvocationCounter.increaseCounter();

    retVal = String.format(
      "There are %d concurrent invocations to this endpoint \n",
      concurrentInvocationCounter.getCounter());

    TimeUnit.SECONDS.sleep(3);

    concurrentInvocationCounter.decreaseCounter();

    return retVal;

  }

}
```

125

In our example, we are allowing up to three concurrent invocations to our RESTful web service endpoint; any attempt to invoke the endpoint while there are already three concurrent invocations will fail with a BulkheadException; once the number of concurrent invocations decreases below three, the method can be successfully invoked again.

The following example code illustrates what happens when we generate more concurrent calls than allowed by the @Bulkhead annotation:

```
package com.ensode.fault.toleranceclient;

//imports omitted

@Path("/faulttoleranceclient")
public class FaultToleranceClientService {

  private static final Logger LOGGER =
    Logger.getLogger(FaultToleranceClientService.class.getName());

  @Inject
  @RestClient
  private FaultToleranceExampleResourceClient client;

  @POST
  @Path("semaphorebulkhead")
  public void semaphoreBulkheadClient() throws
    InterruptedException {
    ExecutorService executorService =
      Executors.newFixedThreadPool(4);

    Callable<String> semaphoreBulkheadCallable =
      () -> client.semaphoreBulkHeadDemo();

    List<Future<String>> callResults = executorService.invokeAll(
      List.of(semaphoreBulkheadCallable,semaphoreBulkheadCallable,
        semaphoreBulkheadCallable,semaphoreBulkheadCallable));

    callResults.forEach(fut -> {
      try {
        LOGGER.log(Level.INFO, fut.get());
      } catch (InterruptedException | ExecutionException ex) {
```

```
        LOGGER.log(Level.SEVERE, String.format(
            "%s caught", ex.getClass().getName()), ex);
      }
    });
  }
}
```

With a little help of the Concurrency Utilities API, we spawn four threads, each of which invokes the endpoint on our service annotated with @Bulkhead annotation. Since we specified a maximum of three concurrent invocations, the last invocation will fail with a @BulkheadException, as expected.

---

Typically, there would be multiple concurrent clients making concurrent requests to a service; for simplicity, our example uses a single client generating multiple concurrent invocations to the service.

---

After running our client service, if we take a look at the Payara Micro output, we can verify that the @Bulkhead annotation is working as expected.

2021-10-18T18:20:18.284-0400] [] [INFO] [] [javax.enterprise.system.core] [tid: _ThreadID=89 _ThreadName=payara-executor-service-scheduled-task] [timeMillis: 1634595618284] [levelValue: 800] mp-fault-tolerance-example-client-1.0-SNAPSHOT was successfully deployed in 428 milliseconds.

**[2021-10-18T18:32:40.472-0400] [] [INFO] [] [com.ensode.fault.toleranceclient.FaultToleranceClientService] [tid: _ThreadID=83 _ ThreadName=http-thread-pool::http-listener(1)] [timeMillis: 1634597555867] [levelValue: 800] There are 1 concurrent invocations to this endpoint**

**[2021-10-18T18:32:40.472-0400] [] [INFO] [] [INFO] [] [com.ensode. fault.toleranceclient.FaultToleranceClientService] [tid: _ThreadID=83 _ ThreadName=http-thread-pool::http-listener(1)] [timeMillis: 1634597555867] [levelValue: 800] There are 3 concurrent invocations to this endpoint**

**[2021-10-18T18:32:40.472-0400] [] [INFO] [[] [INFO] [] [com.ensode. fault.toleranceclient.FaultToleranceClientService] [tid: _ThreadID=83 _ ThreadName=http-thread-pool::http-listener(1)] [timeMillis: 1634597555867] [levelValue: 800] There are 2 concurrent invocations to this endpoint**

```
[2021-10-18T18:32:40.472-0400] [] [SEVERE] [] [com.ensode.fault.
toleranceclient.FaultToleranceClientService] [tid: _ThreadID=83 _
ThreadName=http-thread-pool::http-listener(1)] [timeMillis: 1634596360472]
[levelValue: 1000] [[
  java.util.concurrent.ExecutionException caught
java.util.concurrent.ExecutionException: org.eclipse.microprofile.
faulttolerance.exceptions.BulkheadException: No free work or queue space.
```

```
<intermediate stack trace entries removed for brevity>
```

**Caused by: org.eclipse.microprofile.faulttolerance.exceptions. BulkheadException: No free work or queue space.**

By examining the output for Payara Micro, we can see that the first three concurrent invocations succeeded; the fourth one generated a BulkheadExcetpion, as expected.

---

We have no control over thread scheduling; it is instead done by the JVM and/or the underlying operating system; for this reason, the output indicating the number of concurrent invocations may not match our expectations; the line of code sending output to the log file for the third thread was executed before the same line on the second thread; that's why we see log entries indicating 1, 3, and 2 concurrent invocations, as opposed to 1, 2, and 3.

---

# Using Thread Pools for Asynchronous Endpoints

Thread pool style @Bulkhead usage is limited to asynchronous endpoints; as before, we specify the maximum number of concurrent calls allowed for an endpoint via the value attribute of the @Bulkhead annotation; any additional invocations are placed in a thread pool and serviced after the maximum number of concurrent invocations to our endpoint decreases below the specified value. We can specify the maximum number of invocations on the thread pool via the waitingTaskQueue attribute of the @Bulkhead annotation.

The following example illustrates thread pool style @Bulkhead usage:

```
package com.ensode.faulttolerance;

//imports omitted

@RequestScoped
@Path("faulttoleranceexample")
public class FaulToleranceExampleResource {

  @Inject
  private ConcurrentInvocationCounter concurrentInvocationCounter;

  @POST
  @Path("threadpoolbulkhead")
  @Asynchronous
  @Bulkhead(value = 3, waitingTaskQueue = 2)
  @Produces(MediaType.TEXT_PLAIN)
  public CompletionStage<String> threadPoolBulkheadExample(
    @QueryParam("invocationNum") int invocationNum) throws
    InterruptedException {
    String retVal;
    retVal = String.format("Invocation number %d succeeded \n",
            invocationNum);

    TimeUnit.SECONDS.sleep(3);

    return CompletableFuture.completedStage(retVal);
  }

}
```

As indicated by the @Asynchronous annotation, our endpoint is asynchronous; therefore, we can use @Bulkhead thread pool style. In our example, we allow up to three concurrent invocations, as indicated by the value attribute of @Bulkhead; we are also allowing a maximum of two threads in the pool, indicated in the waitingTaskQueue attribute of the annotation.

Generating more than five concurrent requests (the three that are allowed plus the maximum of two allowed in the thread pool) should result in an exception. The following bash script generates six concurrent requests:

```
#!/bin/bash
for i in {1..6}; do
  curl -i -XPOST http://localhost:8080/faulttolerance/webresources/
  faulttoleranceexample/threadpoolbulkhead?invocationNum=$i &
done
```

Executing the preceding script from a bash shell results in the following output:

```
HTTP/1.1 500 Request failed.
Server: Payara Micro #badassfish
Connection: close
Content-Length: 0
X-Frame-Options: SAMEORIGIN

HTTP/1.1 200 OK
Server: Payara Micro #badassfish
Content-Type: text/plain
Content-Length: 31
X-Frame-Options: SAMEORIGIN

Invocation number 4 succeeded
HTTP/1.1 200 OK
Server: Payara Micro #badassfish
Content-Type: text/plain
Content-Length: 31
X-Frame-Options: SAMEORIGIN

Invocation number 3 succeeded
HTTP/1.1 200 OK
Server: Payara Micro #badassfish
Content-Type: text/plain
Content-Length: 31
X-Frame-Options: SAMEORIGIN
```

```
Invocation number 2 succeeded
HTTP/1.1 200 OK
Server: Payara Micro #badassfish
Content-Type: text/plain
Content-Length: 31
X-Frame-Options: SAMEORIGIN

Invocation number 5 succeeded
HTTP/1.1 200 OK
Server: Payara Micro #badassfish
Content-Type: text/plain
Content-Length: 31
X-Frame-Options: SAMEORIGIN

Invocation number 6 succeeded
```

Interestingly enough, the output shows the first request failed and requests 2 to 5 succeeded; this happens because we have no control of thread scheduling; in this case, the first request was processed last, which is why it failed; it also failed immediately, as opposed to the others that took three seconds to process; that is why, even though the first request was executed last, we see its output first.

# Stop Invoking Repeatedly Failing Endpoints

The @CircuitBreaker annotation allows us to stop invoking endpoints that fail past a threshold; by default, if at least 50% of the last 20 invocations to an endpoint fail, then invocations to that method will stop; instead, the MicroProfile runtime will throw a CircuitBreakerOpenException. We can specify the number of invocations used and the ratio of failed requests via the requestVolumeThreshold and failureRatio attributes of @CircutiBreaker, respectively

After a specified delay (defaulting to 500 milliseconds), the circuit is half opened, meaning that number of requests (default of one request) from are allowed to pass through and invoke the operation; if these requests are successful, the circuit is automatically closed, allowing further requests to access the endpoint; if at least one of these requests fails, the circuit is reopened, preventing any further calls to the endpoint.

We can specify the delay to use before half-opening the circuit via the delay attribute of @CircuitBreaker and the unit of time for the delay via its delayUnit attribute; the default unit of time is milliseconds.

The following example illustrates how to use the @CircuitBreaker annotation:

```
package com.ensode.faulttolerance;

//imports omitted

@RequestScoped
@Path("faulttoleranceexample")
public class FaulToleranceExampleResource {

  @Inject
  private ConcurrentInvocationCounter concurrentInvocationCounter;

  @CircuitBreaker(requestVolumeThreshold = 3, failureRatio = .66
    delay = 1, delayUnit = ChronoUnit.SECONDS, successThreshold = 2)
  @POST
  @Produces(MediaType.TEXT_PLAIN)
  @Path("circuitbreaker")
  public String circuitBreakerExample(@QueryParam("success") boolean
  success) {
    if (success == false) {
      throw new RuntimeException("forcing a failure for demo purposes");
    } else {
      return "Call succeeded";
    }
  }

}
```

For illustration purposes, in our example, we are deliberately throwing an exception when we receive a value of false as a query parameter. In our endpoint, we are using the last three invocations to our endpoint to calculate the threshold, as specified by the requestVolumeThreshold attribute to @CircuitBreaker. We specify the ratio of failed calls as .66 via the failureRatio attribute; in this case, since our request volume threshold is 3 and the failure ratio is .66, the circuit will open after two out of three consecutive calls fail.

In our example, we are specifying a delay of one second before we half-open the circuit; the number of seconds is specified in the delay attribute of @CircuitBreaker and the unit of time in the corresponding delayUnit attribute.

Let's now write a client service that sends multiple requests to our endpoint so that we can verify that the @CircuitBreaker annotation is working as expected.

```
package com.ensode.fault.toleranceclient;

//imports omitted

@Path("/faulttoleranceclient")
public class FaultToleranceClientService {

  private static final Logger LOGGER = Logger.getLogger(FaultTolerance
  ClientService.class.getName());

  @Inject
  @RestClient
  private FaultToleranceExampleResourceClient client;

  @POST
  @Path("circuitbreaker")
  public void circuitBreakerClient() throws InterruptedException {

    try {
      LOGGER.log(Level.INFO, client.circuitBreakerExample(true));
    } catch (RuntimeException re) {
      LOGGER.log(Level.SEVERE, re.getMessage());
    }

    try {
      LOGGER.log(Level.INFO, client.circuitBreakerExample(false));
    } catch (RuntimeException re) {
      LOGGER.log(Level.SEVERE, re.getMessage());
    }

    try {
      LOGGER.log(Level.INFO, client.circuitBreakerExample(false));
    } catch (RuntimeException re) {
      LOGGER.log(Level.SEVERE, re.getMessage());
    }
```

```
      //circuit opens
      try {
        LOGGER.log(Level.INFO, client.circuitBreakerExample(true));
        //call fails because the circuit is open
      } catch (CircuitBreakerOpenException e) {
        LOGGER.log(Level.SEVERE, "Circuit breaker is open", e);
      }

      //Wait one second, circuit is now half open, call succeeds.
      TimeUnit.SECONDS.sleep(1);
      try {
        LOGGER.log(Level.INFO, client.circuitBreakerExample(true));
        //call succeeds because the circuit is half open
      } catch (RuntimeException re) {
        LOGGER.log(Level.SEVERE, re.getMessage());
      }
      //circuit breaker is now closed

  }

}
```

Recall that in our service, we are deliberately throwing an exception when it receives a value of false for its success path parameter; as such, the first invocation to the service succeeds, and the next two fail; since we met the threshold of failed requests, the circuit opens.

The next invocation to the service failed, even though we are passing a value of true; the reason it fails is because the circuit breaker is now open. After the specified delay of one second, the circuit breaker is half open; therefore, calls are allowed to reach the endpoint; the last call from our client succeeds. Since we specified a success threshold of 2 via the successThreshold attribute of @CircuitBreaker, at this point, the circuit breaker remains in half-open state; if the next request succeeds, the circuit is then closed; if it fails, it will be opened.

One last thing to mention before moving on, by default, @CircuitBreaker will increase the counter of failed calls if any exception is thrown from the endpoint. If we wish to limit the circuit breaker functionality to a certain set of exceptions, we can do so via the `failOn` attribute of `@CircuitBreaker`; this attribute accepts an array of child classes of `Exception` as its value, for example:

`@CircuitBreker(failOn={ReallyBadException.class, EvenWorseException.class})`

Similarly, we can specify exceptions to ignore via the `skipOn` attribute of `@CircuitBreaker`.

`@CircuitBreaker(skipOn={DumbException.class, IsThisEvenAnIssueException.class})`

# Providing an Alternative Solution When Execution Fails

By default, any exceptions thrown from RESTful web service endpoints result in an exception being thrown in the client; however, we can gracefully recover from errors via the `@Fallback` annotation. When using `@FallBack`, we can specify an alternate method that will be executed instead of the failing endpoint; this method can be specified via the `fallbackMethod` attribute of `@Fallback`, as illustrated in the following example:

```
package com.ensode.faulttolerance;

//imports omitted

@RequestScoped
@Path("faulttoleranceexample")
public class FaulToleranceExampleResource {

  @Fallback(fallbackMethod = "fallbackMethod")
  @POST
  @Produces(MediaType.TEXT_PLAIN)
  @Path("fallback")
  public String fallbackExample(@QueryParam("success") boolean success) {
    if (success == false) {
      throw new RuntimeException(
      "forcing a failure for demo purposes");
    } else {
      return "Call succeeded";
    }
  }
```

```
  private String fallbackMethod(boolean success) {
    return "Something went wrong";
  }

}
```

To specify a fallback method, we simply indicate the method name as a String as the value of the `fallbackMethod` attribute of `@Fallback`; the fallback method must have the same return type and parameters as the potentially failing endpoint; notice in our example, both the method implementing the endpoint and the fallback method return a String and take a single `boolean` as a parameter; in general, the return value and the parameter types of the endpoint and corresponding fallback method must match.

If the endpoint invocation succeeds, then nothing out of the ordinary happens; if it fails, then the fallback method is invoked instead. For instance, if we send a request to the endpoint we defined in our example and that method fails, we will instead get the output from the fallback method.

```
$ curl -XPOST http://localhost:8080/faulttolerance/webresources/
faulttoleranceexample/fallback?success=false
Something went wrong
```

Using a fallback method is great if we wish to implement alternate functionality if our endpoint ends; however, what if instead we would like to get some diagnostic information about the failing endpoint? In that case, we can indicate a fallback handler class via the `value` attribute of `@Fallback`. A fallback handler must be a class implementing the `FallbackHandler` interface; this interface has a single abstract method called `handle()`; this method accepts an instance of `ExecutionContext` as a parameter; we can use this parameter to obtain information about the failing method.

The following example illustrates how to implement a fallback handler:

```
package com.ensode.faulttolerance;

//imports omitted

@Dependent
public class ExampleFallbackHandler
  implements FallbackHandler<String> {

  private static final Logger LOGGER =
    Logger.getLogger(ExampleFallbackHandler.class.getName());
```

```
@Override
public String handle(ExecutionContext ec) {
  Throwable throwable = ec.getFailure();
  Method buggyMethod = ec.getMethod();
  Object[] parameters = ec.getParameters();

  LOGGER.log(Level.SEVERE, String.format(
    "%s thrown when invoking %s method with parameters: %s",
        throwable.getClass().getName(), buggyMethod.getName(),
          Arrays.asList(parameters)));

  return "Something went wrong, check the logs\n";
  }

}
```

Our `FallbackHandler` implementation must be a CDI bean; the easiest way to turn it into one is to use one of the scope annotations; for `FallbackHandler` implementations, it is usually a good idea to use the @Dependent pseudoscope, which will cause the `FallbackHandler` implementation to use the same scope as the RESTful web service utilizing it.

The `FallbackHandler` interface has a generic type argument; its abstract `handle()` method returns the type we specify, which, in our example, is `String`; its `handle()` method is automatically invoked by the MicroProfile runtime; it passes an instance of a class implementing the `ExecutionContext` interface, which we can use to obtain information about the failed invocation. As shown in the example, we can invoke its `getFailure()` method to obtain the `Throwable` (typically an `Exception`) that was thrown from the endpoint.

Additionally, we can invoke `ExecutionContext.getMethod()` to obtain a reference to the method that failed; we can obtain the method name as a `String` by invoking its `getName()` method.

Finally, we can obtain the arguments that were passed to the failing endpoint by invoking the `getParameters()` method on `ExecutionContext`.

Our example sends this information to the Payara Micro log and returns a String to the client.

In order to use our `FallbackHandler` implementation, we need to specify it as the value of the `@Fallback` annotation in the method implementing the endpoint, as illustrated in the following example:

```
package com.ensode.faulttolerance;

//imports omitted

@RequestScoped
@Path("faulttoleranceexample")
public class FaulToleranceExampleResource {

  @Fallback(ExampleFallbackHandler.class)
  @POST
  @Produces(MediaType.TEXT_PLAIN)
  @Path("fallbackhandler")
  public String fallbackHandlerExample(
    @QueryParam("success") boolean success) {
    if (success == false) {
      throw new RuntimeException(
      "forcing a failure for demo purposes");
    } else {
      return "Call succeeded";
    }
  }

}
```

As seen in the example, all we have to do to defer to a FallbackHandler implementation in case of failure is to add the FallbackHandler class as the value of the `@Fallback` annotation.

If a call to the endpoint fails, our FallbackHandler implementation takes over.

```
$ curl -XPOST http://localhost:8080/faulttolerance/webresources/
faulttoleranceexample/fallbackhandler?success=false
Something went wrong, check the logs
```

If we check the Payara Micro output or log file, we can see the information we retrieved from `ExecutionContext`, which can be used to diagnose and correct the issue.

```
[2021-10-20T14:00:27.797-0400] [] [SEVERE] [] [com.ensode.faulttolerance.
ExampleFallbackHandler] [tid: _ThreadID=77 _ThreadName=http-thread-
pool::http-listener(2)] [timeMillis: 1634752827797] [levelValue: 1000]
```
**java.lang.RuntimeException thrown when invoking fallbackHandlerExample**
**method with parameters: [false]**

By default, @Falback takes over if any exception is thrown from the endpoint. If we
wish to limist the fallback functionality to a certain set of exceptions, we can do so via
the applyOn attribute of @Fallback; this attribute accepts an array of child classes of
Exception as its value, for example:

```
@Fallback(SomeFallBackHandler.class, failOn={ReallyBadException.class,
EvenWorseException.class})
```

Similarly, we can specify exceptions to ignore via the skipOn attribute of @Fallback.

```
@FallBack(fallbackMethod="someMethod", skipOn={DumbException.class,
IsThisEvenAnIssueException.class})
```

# Retrying Execution in Case of Failure

We can use the @Retry annotation to automatically retry an endpoint invocation that
fails, as illustrated in the following example:

```
package com.ensode.faulttolerance;

//imports omitted

@RequestScoped
@Path("faulttoleranceexample")
public class FaulToleranceExampleResource {

  private static final Logger LOGGER = Logger.getLogger
    (FaulToleranceExampleResource.class.getName());

  @Inject
  private EndpointSuccessDeterminator endpointSuccessDeterminator;
```

```java
@Retry
@GET
@Produces(MediaType.TEXT_PLAIN)
@Path("retry")
public String retryExample() {
  LOGGER.log(Level.INFO, "retryExample() invoked");
  boolean success;

  success = endpointSuccessDeterminator.
    allowEndpointToSucceed();

  if (!success) {
    LOGGER.log(
      Level.SEVERE, "retryExample() invocation failed");
    throw new RuntimeException(
      "forcing a failure for demo purposes");
  } else {
    LOGGER.log(Level.INFO,
      "retryExample() invocation succeeded");
    return "Call succeeded\n";
  }
 }

}
```

In our example, we are using an application scoped CDI bean to force our endpoint to fail every other invocation; the bean simply returns a boolean value and flips the value of the boolean after each invocation.

```java
package com.ensode.faulttolerance;

import javax.enterprise.context.ApplicationScoped;

@ApplicationScoped
public class EndpointSuccessDeterminator {

  private boolean successIndicator = true;
```

```
public boolean allowEndpointToSucceed() {
  successIndicator = !successIndicator;

  return successIndicator;
 }

}
```

We use this bean in our endpoint to force a failure so that we can demonstrate the @Retry annotation in action.

If we send an HTTP GET request to our endpoint, nothing looks out of the ordinary.

```
$ curl http://localhost:8080/faulttolerance/webresources/
faulttoleranceexample/retry
Call succeeded
```

However, if we look at the Payara Micro output, we can see that the first invocation failed, it was automatically retried, and the second invocation succeeded.

```
[2021-10-21T14:25:22.034-0400] [] [INFO] [] [com.ensode.faulttolerance.
FaulToleranceExampleResource] [tid: _ThreadID=78 _ThreadName=http-thread-
pool::http-listener(2)] [timeMillis: 1634840722034] [levelValue: 800]
retryExample() invoked

[2021-10-21T14:25:22.035-0400] [] [SEVERE] [] [com.ensode.faulttolerance.
FaulToleranceExampleResource] [tid: _ThreadID=78 _ThreadName=http-thread-
pool::http-listener(2)] [timeMillis: 1634840722035] [levelValue: 1000]
retryExample() invocation failed

[2021-10-21T14:25:22.130-0400] [] [INFO] [] [com.ensode.faulttolerance.
FaulToleranceExampleResource] [tid: _ThreadID=78 _ThreadName=http-thread-
pool::http-listener(2)] [timeMillis: 1634840722130] [levelValue: 800]
retryExample() invoked

[2021-10-21T14:25:22.131-0400] [] [INFO] [] [com.ensode.faulttolerance.
FaulToleranceExampleResource] [tid: _ThreadID=78 _ThreadName=http-thread-
pool::http-listener(2)] [timeMillis: 1634840722131] [levelValue: 800]
retryExample() invocation succeeded
```

The @Retry annotation provides a few attributes we can use to control things like how long to retry, how many times to retry, etc. Table 7-1 lists all attributes for @Retry.

*Table 7-1.* *@Retry Annotation Attributes*

| Attribute | Description | Default |
|---|---|---|
| abortOn | An array of Throwable types that should not trigger a retry | |
| Delay | The delay between retries | 0 |
| delayUnit | The unit of time for the delay attribute | ChronoUnit.MILLIS (milliseconds) |
| durationUnit | The unit of time for the maxDuration attribute | ChronoUnit.MILLIS (milliseconds) |
| Jitter | Used to randomly vary retry delays. Actual delay will be [delay - jitter, delay + jitter] | 200 |
| jitterDelayUnit | The unit of time for the jitter attribute | ChronoUnit.MILLIS (milliseconds) |
| maxDuration | Specifies how long to retry for | 180000 (when combined with the default durationUnit of milliseconds, this is equivalent to three minutes) |
| maxRetries | The maximum number of times to retry, a value of -1 indicates no maximum (retry forever) | 3 |
| retryOn | An array of Throwable types that should trigger a retry | java.lang.Exception |

# Defining a Maximum Duration for Execution

MicroProfile Fault Tolerance provides a @Timeout annotation we can use to specify the maximum time to allow a RESTful web service endpoint to execute. If the method takes longer than the specified amount of time, a TimeoutException is thrown.

The following example illustrates how to use the @Timeout annotation:

```
package com.ensode.faulttolerance;

//imports omitted

@RequestScoped
@Path("faulttoleranceexample")
public class FaulToleranceExampleResource {

  private static final Logger LOGGER = Logger.getLogger(FaulTolerance
  ExampleResource.class.getName());

  @Timeout(value = 3, unit = ChronoUnit.SECONDS)
  @GET
  @Produces(MediaType.TEXT_PLAIN)
  @Path("timeout")
  public String timeoutExample(@QueryParam("delay") long delay) {
    try {
      TimeUnit.SECONDS.sleep(delay);
    } catch (InterruptedException ex) {
      LOGGER.log(Level.INFO, "sleep() interrupted");
    }
    return "Call returned successfully\n";
  }

}
```

In our example, we are specifying that our RESTful web service endpoint should not take more than three seconds to execute, as can be seen in the example, how long to wait before a timeout is specified by combining the value and unit attributes of @Timeout, with the former containing a long value and the latter containing the unit of time. Default values for value and unit are 1000L and ChronoUnit.MILLIS (milliseconds), for a default timeout value of one second. In our example, we are simply suspending execution for the amount of seconds received as a query parameter; this way, we can force the endpoint to time out so that we can see it in action.

If we pass a value of 4 as a query parameter to our endpoint, we can see the @Timeout annotation in action.

```
$ curl -i http://localhost:8080/faulttolerance/webresources/
faulttoleranceexample/timeout?delay=4
HTTP/1.1 500 Internal Server Error
Content-Language:
Content-Type: text/html
Connection: close
Content-Length: 1494
X-Frame-Options: SAMEORIGIN

<!DOCTYPE html PUBLIC "-//W3C//DTD XHTML 1.0 Strict//EN" "http://
www.w3.org/TR/xhtml1/DTD/xhtml1-strict.dtd"><html xmlns="http://www.
w3.org/1999/xhtml"><head><title>Payara Micro #badassfish - Error report
</title><style type="text/css"><!--H1 {font-family:Tahoma,Arial,
sans-serif;color:white;background-color:#525D76;font-size:22px;} H2 {font-
family:Tahoma,Arial,sans-serif;color:white;background-color:#525D76;
font-size:16px;} H3 {font-family:Tahoma,Arial,sans-serif;color:white;
background-color:#525D76;font-size:14px;} BODY {font-family:Tahoma,
Arial,sans-serif;color:black;background-color:white;} B {font-family:
Tahoma,Arial,sans-serif;color:white;background-color:#525D76;}
P {font-family:Tahoma,Arial,sans-serif;background:white;color:black;
font-size:12px;}A {color : black;}HR {color : #525D76;}--></style>
</head><body><h1>HTTP Status 500 - Internal Server Error</h1><hr/><p>
<b>type</b> Exception report</p><p><b>message</b>Internal Server Error</p>
<p><b>description</b>The server encountered an internal error that
prevented it from fulfilling this request.</p><p><b>exception</b>
<pre>javax.servlet.ServletException: org.eclipse.microprofile.
faulttolerance.exceptions.TimeoutException</pre></p><p><b>root cause</b>
<pre>org.eclipse.microprofile.faulttolerance.exceptions.TimeoutException
</pre></p><p><b>note</b> <u>The full stack traces of the exception and its
root causes are available in the Payara Micro #badassfish logs.</u>
</p><hr/><h3>Payara Micro #badassfish</h3></body></html>
```

As we can see from the output of the `curl` command, we receive an HTTP error 500; the response body we receive is automatically generated by Payara Micro; by examining the output, we can see that a `TimeoutException` was thrown; this is the expected behavior since the endpoint took longer than the specified timeout of three seconds.

If the method takes less than the specified timeout value (three seconds, in our example), then the method executes normally.

```
$ curl -i  http://localhost:8080/faulttolerance/webresources/
faulttoleranceexample/timeout?delay=2
HTTP/1.1 200 OK
Server: Payara Micro #badassfish
Content-Type: text/plain
Content-Length: 27
X-Frame-Options: SAMEORIGIN

Call returned successfully
```

# Summary

In this chapter, we covered Payara Micro's support for the MicroProfile Fault Tolerance API.

We discussed how to make RESTful web services asynchronous so that clients don't have to block waiting for them to return.

We also saw how we can limit the number of concurrent executions of a RESTful service endpoint, preventing a buggy or malicious client from overloading the system.

Additionally, we covered how to transparently stop invocations to an endpoint that keeps repeatedly failing.

Also, we saw how we can automatically invoke a fallback implementation when a RESTful web service fails.

Additionally, we saw how to automatically retry failed RESTful service endpoint invocations; lastly, we covered how to specify the maximum amount of time we allow an endpoint to execute before it times out.

# CHAPTER 8

# Health Checks

It is common for cloud-based applications to provide a health check endpoint for orchestration tools such as Kubernetes to use to verify that services are up and running. These orchestration tools can use these endpoints to determine if a service needs to be restarted or otherwise dealt with.

MicroProfile provides a Health Check API we can use to develop these health check endpoints. We can provide reports to determine if the application is live and/or if it is ready. In both cases, we do so by implementing the HealthCheck interface provided by MicroProfile, which provides a single abstract call() method that takes no arguments and returns an instance of HealthCheckResponse; our HealthCheck implementation needs to be an application scoped CDI bean. For basic health check reports, however, we don't actually have to do anything; a default health check endpoint is provided "for free."

## Free Health Check Functionality

By deploying any web application to Payara Micro, we get a basic health check "for free" with no effort whatsoever on our part. Just send an HTTP GET request to the /health context root or the Payara Micro, and we'll get a basic status report in JSON format.

```
$ curl http://localhost:8080/health
{"status":"UP","checks":[]}
```

The default health check response reports that the application is up and provides no additional checks. In many cases, the default health check suffices; if we need to provide additional information, we can do so by utilizing the MicroProfile health check API.

147

© David R. Heffelfinger 2022
D. R. Heffelfinger, *Payara Micro Revealed*, https://doi.org/10.1007/978-1-4842-8161-1_8

# Determining If a Service Is Live

To provide a report indicating if our application is live, we need to annotate our HealthCheck implementation with @Livenesscheck, as illustrated in the following example:

```
package com.ensode.healthcheck;

//imports omitted

@ApplicationScoped
@Liveness
public class LivenessChecker implements HealthCheck {

  @Override
  public HealthCheckResponse call() {
    return HealthCheckResponse.builder().
      name(this.getClass().getSimpleName()).up().build();
  }
}
```

As can be seen in the example, the easiest way to create the HealthCheckResponse instance to return is by using HealthCheckResponseBuilder. The HealthCheckResponse class provides a static builder() method we can use to obtain an instance of HealthCheckResponseBuilder.

We need to provide a name for our health check; we can do so by invoking the name() method on HealthCheckResponseBuilder; the name can be any arbitrary string; in our example, we are using the name of our class.

We indicate if the service is live or not by invoking HealthCheckResponseBuilder. up() or HealthCheckResponseBuilder.down(); in our example, we are simply invoking up(); in a real application, we would perform some logic to determine if the service is up or down and then call the appropriate method. We could also provide additional diagnostic data by invoking HealthCheckResponseBuilder.withData() (more on that later).

Once we are done building our HealthCheckResponse object, we invoke HealthCheckResponseBuilder.build() to create it; then our call() method can simply return it.

Once we are done implementing our liveness check, we can see it in action by submitting an HTTP GET request to the /health endpoint of our application.

```
$ curl http://localhost:8080/health/
{"status":"UP","checks":[{"name":"LivenessChecker","status":"UP",
"data":{}}]}
```

# Determining If a Service Is Ready

A service could be up but not ready to be used; some of its dependencies, for instance, could be down or otherwise unavailable. We can implement health check logic to generate a readiness report by developing a HealthCheck implementation annotated with the @ReadinessCheck annotation.

The process to generate a readiness report is very similar to what we already saw when discussing liveness; we implement the HealthCheck interface and return an instance of HealthCheckResponse from its call() method.

The following example illustrates how we can provide additional data in our health check reports; in this example, we are simulating checking the status of resources our application depends on and returning a status of "up" or "down" as appropriate. Although we are illustrating adding additional data in a readiness example, the material is also applicable to liveness reports.

```
package com.ensode.healthcheck;

//imports omitted

@ApplicationScoped
@Readiness
public class ReadinessChecker implements HealthCheck {

  HealthCheckResponseBuilder healthCheckResponseBuilder =
    HealthCheckResponse.builder().
    name(this.getClass().getSimpleName());

  @Override
  public HealthCheckResponse call() {
```

```
    boolean databaseUp = isDatabaseUp();
    boolean jmsQueuesUp = areJmsQueuesUp();

    if (databaseUp && jmsQueuesUp) {
      healthCheckResponseBuilder =
        healthCheckResponseBuilder.up();
    } else {
      healthCheckResponseBuilder =
        healthCheckResponseBuilder.down();
    }

    return healthCheckResponseBuilder.
      withData("Database up", databaseUp).
      withData("JMS queue up", jmsQueuesUp).build();
  }

  private boolean isDatabaseUp() {
    //dummy method for illustration purposes
    return new Random().nextBoolean();
  }

  private boolean areJmsQueuesUp() {
    //dummy method for illustration purposes
    return new Random().nextBoolean();
  }

}
```

In our example, we create an instance of HealthCheckResponseBuilder and give it a name and then call some methods that simulate checking the status of a database and JMS queue (our dummy methods simply return a random true/false boolean value); if both the database and JMS queue are up, we indicate that the service is ready by invoking HealthCheckResponseBuilder.up(); otherwise, we indicate that the service is not ready by invoking HealthCheckResponseBuilder.down(); simply indicating that the service is not ready would not provide enough information; ideally, we need to indicate why the service is not ready; we can do so by invoking HealthCheckResponseBuilder. withData(); there are three overloaded versions of this method; all three take a string as its first argument; the second argument can be another string, a long or a boolean.

The first argument is meant to provide a brief description for the generated data; the second value is the actual value to be displayed; in our example, we are using the boolean version of withData() indicating if the database and JMS queues are up.

If we have both liveness and readiness checks in our application, sending an HTTP GET request to our application will generate data for both checks.

curl http://localhost:8080/health/ generates the following output (reformatted for readability):

```
{
    "status": "UP",
    "checks": [
      {
        "name": "ReadinessChecker",
        "status": "UP",
        "data": {
          "Database up": "true",
          "JMS queue up": "true"
        }
      },
      {
        "name": "LivenessChecker",
        "status": "UP",
        "data": {}
      }
    ]
}
```

If we want to see only the readiness check, we can invoke the /health/ready endpoint; for instance, curl http://localhost:8080/health/ready generates the following output:

```
{
  "status": "UP",
  "checks": [
    {
      "name": "ReadinessChecker",
      "status": "UP",
```

```
    "data": {
       "Database up": "true",
       "JMS queue up": "true"
    }
  }
 ]
}
```

Similarly, if we only want to see a liveness report, we can send an HTTP GET request to /health/live, which will result in a JSON response containing the liveness check only.

```
{
  "status": "UP",
  "checks": [
    {
      "name": "LivenessChecker",
      "status": "UP",
      "data": {}
    }
  ]
}
```

# Configuring MicroProfile Health

We can configure MicroProfile Health in Payara Micro via the set-microprofile-healthcheck-configuration asadmin command via a command file passed as a post boot command file or similar.

# Disabling MicroProfile Health

Payara Micro enables MicroProfile Health by default; if we wish to disable it, we can use the following asadmin command:

```
set-microprofile-healthcheck-configuration --enabled=false
```

## Securing MicroProfile Health

By default, the *//health* endpoint is unsecured, meaning any random unauthenticated user can access it.

If we wish to secure it, we can do so by issuing the following asadmin command:

```
set-microprofile-healthcheck-configuration --securityenabled=true
```

When securing the */health* endpoint, we can specify which roles have access to it as follows:

```
set-microprofile-healthcheck-configuration --roles=role1,role2
```

The value of the `--roles` argument is a comma-separated list of roles allowed to access the health endpoint.

## Customizing the MicroProfile Health Endpoint

By default, metrics can be retrieved via the */health* endpoint. We can use a different endpoint if we wish.

```
set-microprofile-healthcheck-configuration --endpoint=foo
```

The value of the *--endpoint* argument is the context root of our custom health endpoint.

# Summary

In this chapter, we covered Payara Micro's support for the MicroProfile Health API. We saw how we get basic health functionality "for free"; we also covered how to generate custom health data to help determine if a service is ready and/or live. Finally, we covered how to configure MicroProfile Health in Payara Micro.

# CHAPTER 9

# Request Tracing

A typical microservices architecture consists of several microservices. These services send output to a log file; traditionally, each service sends output to its own log file. When looking at log files across server instances, it is almost never trivial to follow a single trace of execution across our microservices; for example, let's say we have two services, A and B, and that service A serves as a client for service B. Typically, we will see several calls to service B from service A in the logs, but it is seldom trivial to match which calls from service A match which calls received from service B. Additionally, it is possible service B may be called from clients other than service A, making following a single trace of execution in our application a challenging task. This is where the MicroProfile OpenTracing API comes in; this API generates spans and traces that allow us to trace execution across Payara Micro instances; each span and trace has a unique ID that does not change across instances, allowing us to link log entries from one instance of Payara Micro to another.

Before we can use the MicroProfile OpenTracing API, it needs to be enabled in Payara Micro.

## Enabling Request Tracing in Payara Micro

The easiest way to enable request tracing in Payara Micro is via the `--enableRequest Tracing` command line argument, for example:

```
java -jar payara-micro-5.2021.8.jar --enableRequestTracing --deploy /path/
to/my.war
```

By default, any request taking longer than 30 seconds will be traced. Output is sent to the Payara Micro console in JSON format.

© David R. Heffelfinger 2022
D. R. Heffelfinger, *Payara Micro Revealed*, https://doi.org/10.1007/978-1-4842-8161-1_9

If we wish to override the default minimum amount of time a request must take before it is traced, we can do so via the --thresholdValue and --thresholdUnit command-line arguments, for example, to trace any request taking longer than 100 milliseconds:

```
java -jar payara-micro-5.2021.8.jar --enableRequestTracing --requestTracing
ThresholdValue 100 --requestTracingThresholdUnit milliseconds --deploy /
path/to/my.war
```

The --requestTracingThresholdUnit command-line argument accepts the following time units:

- NANOSECONDS
- MICROSECONDS
- MILLISECONDS
- SECONDS
- MINUTES
- HOURS
- DAYS

---

All values for --requestTracingThresholdUnit are case insensitive.

---

Additionally, --enableRequestTracing accepts an optional value indicating the minimum amount of time a request must take in order to be traced, for example:

```
java -jar payara-micro-5.2021.8.jar --enableRequestTracing 100ms --deploy /
path/to/my.war
```

The preceding command is an alternative way to configure request tracing so that any request taking longer than 100 milliseconds is traced. The optional value of --enableRequestTracing must be an integer value followed by a unit of time, *without any spaces between them.*

Valid values for units of time could be the spelled-out unit of time (i.e., "nanoseconds"), or the equivalent abbreviation (i.e., "ns").

Table 9-1 lists valid values for the unit of time portion of the `--enableRequest`
`Tracing` optional parameter.

***Table 9-1.*** *Request Tracing Units of Time*

| Unit of Time | Spelled-Out Value (Case Insensitive) | Abbreviated Value |
|---|---|---|
| Nanoseconds | nanoseconds | ns |
| Microseconds | microseconds | us or µs |
| Milliseconds | milliseconds | ms |
| Seconds | seconds | s |
| Minutes | minutes | m |
| Hours | hours | h |
| Days | days | d |

All spelled-out values also accept their singular counterparts (nanosecond,
microsecond, etc.).

# Spans and Traces

A *span* represents an individual unit of work, typically a single HTTP request; by default,
Payara Micro logs spans in JSON format to its console output.

A *trace* is a collection of related spans; for example, we could send an HTTP
request to a microservice, which in turn sends two more requests to two additional
microservices; all three requests in this case would have unique span IDs, but all
would share the same trace ID; by looking at the trace ID of each span, we can find
out which requests are related. Trace IDs are unique and match even across Payara
Micro instances, making it possible to relate log entries in one Payara Micro instance to
another.

Let's look at an example; when discussing programmatic application metrics in Chapter 6, we developed a service to hire or fire employees; additionally, we developed a client service that would hire three employees from a single endpoint; for reference, here is the relevant code for the service implementing the logic to hire employees (metrics specific code removed for simplicity):

```
package com.ensode.requesttracing;

//imports omitted

@ApplicationScoped
@Path("employeeservice")
public class EmployeeResource {

  private List<Employee> employeeList = new CopyOnWriteArrayList<>();
//thread safe

  @PUT
  @Consumes(MediaType.APPLICATION_JSON)
  public void hireEmployee(Employee employee) throws InterruptedException {
    //simulate slow processing
    Thread.sleep(100);
    employeeList.add(employee);
  }
}
```

---

To slow down processing a bit and make sure our `hireEmployee()` method gets traces, we added a 100-ms delay to the method.

---

Via the MicroProfile REST client API, the client service sends three HTTP PUT requests to the preceding service, generating three related HTTP requests.

```
package com.ensode.requesttracing.client;

//imports omitted
@ApplicationScoped
@Path("employeeclient")
public class EmployeeClientResource {
```

```
@Inject
@RestClient
private EmployeeResourceClient employeeResourceClient;

private List<Employee> employeesToHire;

@PostConstruct
public void init() {
  Employee employee1 = new Employee("Jose", "Jimenez");
  Employee employee2 = new Employee("Meera", "Patel");
  Employee employee3 = new Employee("David", "Heffelfinger");

  employeesToHire = List.of(employee1, employee2, employee3);

}

@Path("hire")
@POST
public void hireEmployees() {
  employeesToHire.forEach(emp ->
    employeeResourceClient.hireEmployee(emp));
}

}
```

If we enable request tracing with a threshold of 100 ms and send an HTTP POST request to http://localhost:8081/requesttracingclient/webresources/employeeclient/hire, we can see all generated spans on the Payara Micro output for both instances of Payara Micro: the one running the employee client service and the one running the employee service.

On the employee client service Payara Micro instance, we would see output similar to the following:

```
[2021-11-12T13:18:40.472-0500] [] [INFO] [] [fish.payara.nucleus.
notification.log.LogNotifier] [tid: _ThreadID=89 _ThreadName=log-
notifier-1] [timeMillis: 1636741120472] [levelValue: 800] [[
  Request execution time: 914(ms) exceeded the acceptable threshold -
{"traceSpans":[
```

{"operationName":"processContainerRequest","spanContext":{"spanId":
"e6749770-ab55-4260-887f-520997aab357","traceId":"10b36dfc-30ed-4f26-bf7f-
c73d3d4bdb6f"},"startTime":"2021-11-12T13:18:39.554501-05:00[America/New_York]",
"endTime":"2021-11-12T13:18:40.469-05:00[America/New_York]","traceDuration"
:"914499000","spanTags":[{"Server": "server"},{"Domain": "domain1"}]},
{"operationName":"processWebserviceRequest","spanContext":{"spanId":"4661ad
ac-0ae8-4a97-a303-8eae965fa8f0","traceId":"10b36dfc-30ed-4f26-bf7f-
c73d3d4bdb6f"},"startTime":"2021-11-12T13:18:39.594981-05:00[America/New_York]",
"endTime":"2021-11-12T13:18:40.468138-05:00[America/New_York]","trace
Duration":"873154000","spanTags":[{"ResponseStatus": "204"},{"host":
"[localhost:8081]"},{"Method": "POST"},{"URL": "http://localhost:8081/
requesttracingclient/webresources/employeeclient/hire"},{"user-agent":
"[curl/7.68.0]"},{"accept": "[*/*]"}],"references":[{"spanContext":{"spanId"
:"e6749770-ab55-4260-887f-520997aab357","traceId":"10b36dfc-30ed-4f26-bf7f-
c73d3d4bdb6f"},"relationshipType":"ChildOf"}]}, {"operationName":"POST:com.
ensode.requesttracing.client.EmployeeClientResource.hireEmployees","spanCon
text":{"spanId":"6ae72f1e-a103-4f26-9945-a4b35bbcc49a","traceId":"10b36d
fc-30ed-4f26-bf7f-c73d3d4bdb6f"},"startTime":"2021-11-12T13:18:39.643-05:00
[America/New_York]","endTime":"2021-11-12T13:18:40.467588-05:00[America/
New_York]","traceDuration":"824584000","spanTags":[{"http.status_code":
"204"},{"component": "jaxrs"},{"span.kind": "server"},{"http.url":
"http://localhost:8081/requesttracingclient/webresources/employeeclient/
hire"},{"http.method": "POST"}],"references":[{"spanContext":{"spanId":
"4661adac-0ae8-4a97-a303-8eae965fa8f0","traceId":"10b36dfc-30ed-4f26-bf7f-
c73d3d4bdb6f"},"relationshipType":"ChildOf"}]}, {"operationName":"PUT","spa
nContext":{"spanId":"82ce9de2-239c-4854-aa07-ff2f7c2b388e","traceId":"10b36
dfc-30ed-4f26-bf7f-c73d3d4bdb6f"},"startTime":"2021-11-12T13:18:39.887-05:0
0[America/New_York]","endTime":"2021-11-12T13:18:40.244796-05:00[America/
New_York]","traceDuration":"357791000","spanTags":[{"http.status_code":
"204"},{"component": "jaxrs"},{"span.kind": "client"},{"http.url": "http://
localhost:8080/requesttracing/webresources/employeeservice"},{"http.method":
"PUT"}],"references":[{"spanContext":{"spanId":"6ae72f1e-a103-4f26-9945-
a4b35bbcc49a","traceId":"10b36dfc-30ed-4f26-bf7f-c73d3d4bdb6f"},"relationshipType":"ChildOf"}]}, {"operationName":"PUT","spanContext":{"spanId":"
715d1e55-82de-4176-82b2-d0bd5309d315","traceId":"10b36dfc-30ed-4f26-bf7f-

c73d3d4bdb6f"},"startTime":"2021-11-12T13:18:40.248-05:00[America/New_York]",
"endTime":"2021-11-12T13:18:40.357046-05:00[America/New_York]","trace
Duration":"109037000","spanTags":[{"http.status_code": "204"},{"component":
"jaxrs"},{"span.kind": "client"},{"http.url": "http://localhost:8080/
requesttracing/webresources/employeeservice"},{"http.method": "PUT"}],
"references":[{"spanContext":{"spanId":"6ae72f1e-a103-4f26-9945-a4b3
5bbcc49a","traceId":"10b36dfc-30ed-4f26-bf7f-c73d3d4bdb6f"},"relationshipType":
"ChildOf"}]}, {"operationName":"PUT","spanContext":{"spanId":
"f026af13-61cc-4767-bfc6-c123eb142ac5","traceId":"10b36dfc-30ed-4f26-bf7f-
c73d3d4bdb6f"},"startTime":"2021-11-12T13:18:40.357-05:00[America/New_York]",
"endTime":"2021-11-12T13:18:40.463478-05:00[America/New_York]","trace
Duration":"106473000","spanTags":[{"http.status_code": "204"},{"component":
"jaxrs"},{"span.kind": "client"},{"http.url": "http://localhost:8080/
requesttracing/webresources/employeeservice"},{"http.method": "PUT"}],
"references":[{"spanContext":{"spanId":"6ae72f1e-a103-4f26-9945-a4b35bbcc49a",
"traceId":"10b36dfc-30ed-4f26-bf7f-c73d3d4bdb6f"},"relationshipType":
"ChildOf"}]}
]}]]

This is JSON-formatted trace with six spans; each span has useful data such as the operation name, span ID, trace ID, start and end times, and trace duration.

---

The first two spans in the output, with operation names of "processContainer Request" and "processWebserviceRequest", are internal Payara Micro calls that get added to the trace.

---

Notice that in the output, each individual span has a unique ID; however, the trace ID is identical in each one of them; this trace ID is what we can use to link individual requests to a single trace of execution.

If we inspect the output of the Payara Micro instance, we can see output similar to the following:

```
[[2021-11-12T13:18:40.234-0500] [] [INFO] [] [fish.payara.nucleus.
notification.log.LogNotifier] [tid: _ThreadID=85 _ThreadName=log-
notifier-1] [timeMillis: 1636741120234] [levelValue: 800] [[
```

Request execution time: 293(ms) exceeded the acceptable threshold -
{"traceSpans":[
{"operationName":"processContainerRequest","spanContext":{"spanId":"d0
7f7f93-17f5-4372-a64f-4501d8c63a62","traceId":"10b36dfc-30ed-4f26-bf7f
-c73d3d4bdb6f"},"startTime":"2021-11-12T13:18:39.936441-05:00[America/
New_York]","endTime":"2021-11-12T13:18:40.230-05:00[America/New_York]","
traceDuration":"293559000","spanTags":[{"Server": "server"},{"Domain":
"domain1"}],"references":[{"spanContext":{"spanId":"e6749770-ab55-4260-887f-
520997aab357","traceId":"10b36dfc-30ed-4f26-bf7f-c73d3d4bdb6f"},"relationship
Type":"ChildOf"}]}, {"operationName":"processWebserviceRequest
","spanContext":{"spanId":"bc56a4e5-3347-42d5-895f-99c2c94cc4cf",
"traceId":"10b36dfc-30ed-4f26-bf7f-c73d3d4bdb6f"},"startTime":"2021-
11-12T13:18:39.983108-05:00[America/New_York]","endTime":"2021-11-1
2T13:18:40.229562-05:00[America/New_York]","traceDuration":"246449000",
"spanTags":[{"traceid": "[a1155558-7068-4c7e-a8b8-2175ba104233]"},{"content-
length": "[41]"},{"Method": "PUT"},{"URL": "http://localhost:8080/
requesttracing/webresources/employeeservice"},{"payara-tracing-traceid":
"[10b36dfc-30ed-4f26-bf7f-c73d3d4bdb6f]"},{"accept": "[application/
json]"},{"payara-tracing-relationshiptype": "[ChildOf]"},{"spanid":
"[82ce9de2-239c-4854-aa07-ff2f7c2b388e]"},{"ResponseStatus":
"204"},{"payara-tracing-parentid": "[e6749770-ab55-4260-887f-520997aa
b357]"},{"host": "[localhost:8080]"},{"content-type": "[application/
json]"},{"connection": "[keep-alive]"},{"user-agent": "[Jersey/2.34.
payara-p1 (HttpUrlConnection 11.0.12)]"}],"references":[{"spanContext":
{"spanId":"d07f7f93-17f5-4372-a64f-4501d8c63a62","traceId":"10b36dfc-30ed-
4f26-bf7f-c73d3d4bdb6f"},"relationshipType":"ChildOf"}]}, {"operationName":
"PUT:com.ensode.requesttracing.EmployeeResource.hireEmployee","spanCont
ext":{"spanId":"19090bd3-6102-40fe-8cf2-b8831a572129","traceId":"10b36d
fc-30ed-4f26-bf7f-c73d3d4bdb6f"},"startTime":"2021-11-12T13:18:40.023-05:
00[America/New_York]","endTime":"2021-11-12T13:18:40.228787-05:00[America/
New_York]","traceDuration":"205780000","spanTags":[{"http.status_code":
"204"},{"component": "jaxrs"},{"span.kind": "server"},{"http.url": "http://
localhost:8080/requesttracing/webresources/employeeservice"},{"http.
method": "PUT"}],"references":[{"spanContext":{"spanId":"82ce9
de2-239c-4854-aa07-ff2f7c2b388e","traceId":"a1155558-7068-4c7e-
a8b8-2175ba104233"},"relationshipType":"ChildOf"},{"spanContext":{"spanId"

:"bc56a4e5-3347-42d5-895f-99c2c94cc4cf","traceId":"10b36dfc-30ed-4f26-bf7f-
c73d3d4bdb6f"},"relationshipType":"ChildOf"}]}
]}]]

In this case, we see only a single HTTP PUT request being traced; the reason we don't see all three HTTP PUT requests is because we specified a threshold of 100 ms for request tracing when we started this instance of Payara Micro; the other two PUT requests took less than 100 ms; therefore, they were not traced. Note that the trace ID matches the value of the corresponding trace ID on the instance running the client service, allowing us to correlate the invocations.

# Customizing Request Tracing

As seen in the previous section, by simply enabling request tracing and specifying a threshold, we get a lot of functionality, which will suffice for most cases. However, we can customize request tracing if the default functionality does not fit our needs.

The MicroProfile OpenTracing API includes a @Traced annotation that allows us to trace methods other than webservice endpoints; it also allows us to disable tracing for any method and to customize the operation name.

We can also further customize request tracing output via the Tracer annotation, which can be used to add additional information to spans, as well as to create additional spans not bound to a method.

## Tracing Additional Methods

We can trace any method on a CDI bean by decorating it with the @Traced annotation.

---

Annotating a CDI bean with @Traced at the class level will result in all methods in the bean being traced.

---

For example, let's say our EmployeeResource service fired a CDI event every time we hired an employee; we could have the method observing the event be traced by annotating it with @Traced.

```
package com.ensode.requesttracing;
```

```
//imports omitted

@ApplicationScoped
public class EmployeeEventHandler {

  private static final Logger LOGGER =
    Logger.getLogger(EmployeeEventHandler.class.getName());

  @Traced
  public void handleEmployeeEvent(@Observes Employee employee)
    LOGGER.log(Level.INFO,
      String.format("Hired %s %s",
      employee.getFirstName(), employee.getLastName()));
  }
}
```

The *@Traced* annotation would add a new span to the generated trace.

[2021-11-12T15:15:51.189-0500] [] [INFO] [] [fish.payara.nucleus.
notification.log.LogNotifier] [tid: _ThreadID=84 _ThreadName=log-
notifier-1] [timeMillis: 1636748151189] [levelValue: 800] [[
  Request execution time: 208(ms) exceeded the acceptable threshold -
{"traceSpans":[
{"operationName":"processContainerRequest","spanContext":{"spanId":"a4cdd77f-
edfd-4e88-8d23-ffe37f2bd8d0","traceId":"7ebf04e9-1a62-494e-867c-cd80cefa31d9"
},"startTime":"2021-11-12T15:15:50.977342-05:00[America/New_York]","endTime"
:"2021-11-12T15:15:51.186-05:00[America/New_York]","traceDuration":"20865800
0","spanTags":[{"Server": "server"},{"Domain": "domain1"}],"references":[{"
spanContext":{"spanId":"1d842a34-6b2b-43f2-a9b0-1dcb4c1b8629","traceId":"7e
bf04e9-1a62-494e-867c-cd80cefa31d9"},"relationshipType":"ChildOf"}]}, {"op
erationName":"processWebserviceRequest","spanContext":{"spanId":"25d4e2
2e-eac2-4425-a274-f8ab703610ff","traceId":"7ebf04e9-1a62-494e-867c-cd80ce
fa31d9"},"startTime":"2021-11-12T15:15:50.977893-05:00[America/New_York]",
"endTime":"2021-11-12T15:15:51.186627-05:00[America/New_York]","traceDura
tion":"208733000","spanTags":[{"traceid": "[b5382f8d-de60-4aa8-9a24-39302
747183b]"},{"content-length": "[47]"},{"Method": "PUT"},{"URL": "http://
localhost:8080/requesttracing/webresources/employeeservice"},{"payara-tracing-
traceid": "[7ebf04e9-1a62-494e-867c-cd80cefa31d9]"},{"accept": "[application/
```
```

json]"},{"payara-tracing-relationshiptype": "[ChildOf]"},{"spanid": "[afdbae15-a93f-49c1-bcec-5e128a47af0d]"},{"ResponseStatus": "204"},{"payara-tracing-parentid": "[1d842a34-6b2b-43f2-a9b0-1dcb4c1b8629]"},{"host": "[localhost:8080]"},{"content-type": "[application/json]"},{"connection": "[keep-alive]"},{"user-agent": "[Jersey/2.34.payara-p1 (HttpUrlConnection 11.0.12)]"}]}, {"operationName":"PUT:com.ensode.requesttracing. EmployeeResource.hireEmployee","spanContext":{"spanId":"c909a5 1d-49dc-4882-8a20-ba399d23db01","traceId":"7ebf04e9-1a62-494e-867c-cd80c efa31d9"},"startTime":"2021-11-12T15:15:50.981-05:00[America/New_York]", "endTime":"2021-11-12T15:15:51.186518-05:00[America/New_York]","traceDur ation":"205514000","spanTags":[{"http.status_code": "204"},{"component": "jaxrs"},{"span.kind": "server"},{"http.url": "http://localhost:8080/ requesttracing/webresources/employeeservice"},{"employee": "David Heffelfinger"},{"http.method": "PUT"}],"references":[{"spanContext":{"spanId" :"afdbae15-a93f-49c1-bcec-5e128a47af0d","traceId":"b5382f8d-de60-4aa8-9a24-39302747183b"},"relationshipType":"ChildOf"},{"spanContext":{"spanId": "25d4e22e-eac2-4425-a274-f8ab703610ff","traceId":"7ebf04e9-1a62-494e-867c-c-d80ce[a31d9"},"relationshipType":"ChildOf"}]}, **{"operationName":"com. ensode.requesttracing.EmployeeEventHandler.handleEmployeeEvent","spanCo ntext":{"spanId":"3142e614-7203-4b5e-9c94-06979c031f89","traceId":"7ebf 04e9-1a62-494e-867c-cd80cefa31d9"},"startTime":"2021-11-12T15:15:51.085-05: 00[America/New_York]","endTime":"2021-11-12T15:15:51.185988-05:00[America/ New_York]","traceDuration":"100983000","references":[{"spanContext":{ "spanId":"c909a51d-49dc-4882-8a20-ba399d23db01","traceId":"7ebf04e9-1a62-494e-867c-cd80cefa31d9"},"relationshipType":"ChildOf"}]}**
]}]]

## Disabling Request Tracing

We can disable tracing of any web service endpoint by simply annotating it with @Traced(false), for example, in the hireEmployee() method of EmployeeResource:

```
@Traced(false)
@PUT
@Consumes(MediaType.APPLICATION_JSON)
public void hireEmployee(Employee employee)
```

```
  throws InterruptedException {
   //simulate slow processing
   Thread.sleep(100);

   employeeList.add(employee);
   employeeEvent.fire(employee);
 }
```

# Customizing the Operation Name

By default, the generated operation name in a span is the fully qualified name of the method being invoked (if the method was invoked as the direct result of an HTTP request, then the method name is preceded by the HTTP request type (PUT, GET, POST, etc.).

If we wish to customize the operation name displayed on the span, we can do so by setting the operationName attribute on the @Traced annotation; for example, in the hireEmployee() method of EmployeeResource, we could do the following:

```
@Traced(operationName = "employeeHire")
@PUT
@Consumes(MediaType.APPLICATION_JSON)
public void hireEmployee(Employee employee)
  throws InterruptedException {
  //simulate slow processing
  Thread.sleep(100);

  employeeList.add(employee);
  employeeEvent.fire(employee);
}
```

which would result in the following output in the Payara Micro console (for brevity, only the relevant span is shown):

**{"operationName":"employeeHire"**,"spanContext":{"spanId":"764
7b911-4999-48ad-9c7b-a4eb87629a89","traceId":"1d50764c-848c-4f59-
aa7e-902df1813fd8"},"startTime":"2021-11-12T15:31:21.145-05:00[America/
New_York]","endTime":"2021-11-12T15:31:21.352779-05:00[America/New_York]",
"traceDuration":"207775000","spanTags":[{"http.status_code":

"204"},{"component": "jaxrs"},{"span.kind": "server"},{"http.url": "http://localhost:8080/requesttracing/webresources/employeeservice"},{"http.method": "PUT"}],"references":[{"spanContext":{"spanId":"c8fbdf31-744a-455a-80c3-2488a8c5c1e9","traceId":"b45f2bd3-762f-42e5-9950-9553c05b67f8"},"relationshipType":"ChildOf"},{"spanContext":{"spanId":"46a5c1c2-4ae0-4395-ad6d-c2bc7fe03808","traceId":"1d50764c-848c-4f59-aa7e-902df1813fd8"},"relationshipType":"ChildOf"}]}

## Adding Additional Information to Spans

Another way we can customize spans is by adding custom tags to the generated JSON strings. To do this, we need to add an additional dependency for the OpenTracing API; when using Maven, we can do this by adding an additional <dependency> tag to our *pom.xml* file, as in the following example (for brevity, only relevant parts of *pom.xml* are shown):

```xml
<?xml version="1.0" encoding="UTF-8"?>
<project xmlns="http://maven.apache.org/POM/4.0.0" xmlns:xsi="http://www.w3.org/2001/XMLSchema-instance" xsi:schemaLocation="http://maven.apache.org/POM/4.0.0 http://maven.apache.org/xsd/maven-4.0.0.xsd">
  <modelVersion>4.0.0</modelVersion>

  <groupId>com.ensode</groupId>
  <artifactId>request-tracing</artifactId>
  <version>1.0-SNAPSHOT</version>
  <packaging>war</packaging>

  <name>request-tracing</name>

  <dependencyManagement>
    <dependencies>
      <dependency>
        <groupId>fish.payara.api</groupId>
        <artifactId>payara-bom</artifactId>
        <version>${version.payara}</version>
        <type>pom</type>
        <scope>import</scope>
```

```
    </dependency>
  </dependencies>
</dependencyManagement>

<dependencies>
  <!-- additionaldependencies removed for brevity -->
  <dependency>
    <groupId>io.opentracing</groupId>
    <artifactId>opentracing-api</artifactId>
  </dependency>
</dependencies>
</project>
```

Most Maven projects for applications to be deployed to Payara Micro should include the *payara-bom* dependency in its <dependencyManagement> section.

---

A Maven Bill of Materials (BOM) dictates the correct version of dependencies to our project. By using a BOM, we can add a dependency to our project without specifying its version, the correct version that will work with our other dependencies is declared in the BOM.

---

*payara-bom* includes a dependency for opentracing-api in its <dependencyManagement> section; therefore, when adding this dependency to our project, we don't need to specify a version, as seen in the preceding *pom.xml* file.

Once we have added the necessary dependency, we need to inject an instance of io.opentracing.Tracer into our code and use it to add custom tags to our spans.

```
package com.ensode.requesttracing;

import io.opentracing.Tracer;
//additional imports omitted

@ApplicationScoped
@Path("employeeservice")
public class EmployeeResource {

  @Inject
  private Tracer tracer;
```

```
private List<Employee> employeeList = new CopyOnWriteArrayList<>();
//thread safe

@PUT
@Consumes(MediaType.APPLICATION_JSON)
public void hireEmployee(Employee employee) throws InterruptedException {
  //simulate slow processing
  Thread.sleep(100);

  tracer.activeSpan().setTag(
    "employee", String.format("%s %s", employee.getFirstName(),
     employee.getLastName()));
  employeeList.add(employee);
  }
}
```

As we can see in the example, we obtain an instance of io.opentracing.Span representing the current span by invoking Tracer.activeSpan(); from that, we invoke the setTag() method, which has two parameters: a String for the tag name, plus an additional parameter for the value. There are three overloaded versions of setTag(); the second parameter could be a String, a boolean, or a Number (any numeric value); in our example, we used the version with two Strings, since we are adding a tag containing the hired employee's first and last names.

We can see our custom tag by invoking our RESTful web service as usual; our custom tag will be displayed in the JSON string for our span.

{"operationName":"PUT:com.ensode.requesttracing.EmployeeResource.hire
Employee","spanContext":{"spanId":"db583e67-b160-4acd-8e14-1543381848b1",
"traceId":"3410bb5f-016c-45c4-a0ef-fd67124af853"},"startTime":
"2021-11-15T11:33:54.479-05:00[America/New_York]","endTime":"2021-11-1
5T11:33:54.680121-05:00[America/New_York]","traceDuration":"201116000",
"spanTags":[{"http.status_code": "204"},{"component": "jaxrs"},{"span.kind":
"server"},{"http.url": "http://localhost:8080/requesttracing/webresources/
employeeservice"},**{"employee": "Jose Jimenez"}**,{"http.method": "PUT"}],
"references":[{"spanContext":{"spanId":"b7b53629-7890-43d1-9dc4-1c736d21f1cc",
"traceId":"d5d2cca0-b1b4-4688-8c06-f545c256a1be"},"relationshipType":"ChildOf"},
{"spanContext":{"spanId":"42a56b8d-183a-49ef-bc0b-0c322a81930f","traceId":
"3410bb5f-016c-45c4-a0ef-fd67124af853"},"relationshipType":"ChildOf"}]}

# Creating Additional Spans

We can add custom spans to the current trace by invoking `Tracer.buildSpan()`, as illustrated in the following example:

```
package com.ensode.requesttracing;

//imports omitted

@ApplicationScoped
@Path("employeeservice")
public class EmployeeResource

  @Inject
  private Tracer tracer;

  private List<Employee> employeeList = new CopyOnWriteArrayList<>();
  //thread safe

  @PUT
  @Consumes(MediaType.APPLICATION_JSON)
  public void hireEmployee(Employee employee) throws InterruptedException {
    Span customSpan;
    Tracer.SpanBuilder spanBuilder =
      tracer.buildSpan("customSpan");

    customSpan = spanBuilder.start();
    //simulate slow processing
    Thread.sleep(215);
    customSpan.finish();

    employeeList.add(employee);
  }
}
```

`Tracer.buildSpan()` creates an instance of the `SpanBuilder` class, which is an inner class of `Tracer`; this method takes a single argument, a `String` indicating the operation name of our custom span.

When we actually want to start our custom span, we need to invoke the start() method on the SpanBuilder instance we created when invoking buildSpan(); to stop our custom span, we invoke its finish() method; when we execute the endpoint containing our custom tag, we will be able to see it in the Payara Micro console output.

```
[2021-11-15T18:28:23.429-0500] [] [INFO] [] [fish.payara.nucleus.
notification.log.LogNotifier] [tid: _ThreadID=90 _ThreadName=log-
notifier-1] [timeMillis: 1637018903429] [levelValue: 800] [[
  Request execution time: 228(ms) exceeded the acceptable threshold -
{"traceSpans":[
{"operationName":"processContainerRequest","spanContext":{"spanId":"c4d7a6
ab-eb74-4bf1-9b72-db0408cbf782"},"traceId":"0e282189-a825-466e-8488-b2fe569f
7a0f"},"startTime":"2021-11-15T18:28:23.199057-05:00[America/New_York]",
"endTime":"2021-11-15T18:28:23.428-05:00[America/New_York]","traceDuration":
"228943000","spanTags":[{"Server": "server"},{"Domain": "domain1"}],"references":
[{"spanContext":{"spanId":"0e608033-901d-48c5-8d13-839507128e23","traceId":
"0e282189-a825-466e-8488-b2fe569f7a0f"},"relationshipType":"ChildOf"}]},
{"operationName":"processWebserviceRequest","spanContext":{"spanId":"17011bca-
7418-42e6-8513-4a586752fb10","traceId":"0e282189-a825-466e-8488-b2fe569f7a0f"},
"startTime":"2021-11-15T18:28:23.200232-05:00[America/New_York]","endTime":
"2021-11-15T18:28:23.428209-05:00[America/New_York]","traceDuration"
:"227974000","spanTags":[{"traceid": "[2f61f32a-c96d-4521-8a82-64e9779
9f626]"},{"content-length": "[40]"},{"Method": "PUT"},{"URL": "http://
localhost:8080/requesttracing/webresources/employeeservice"},{"payara-
tracing-traceid": "[0e282189-a825-466e-8488-b2fe569f7a0f]"},{"accept":
"[application/json]"},{"payara-tracing-relationshiptype": "[ChildOf]"},
{"spanid": "[922671a9-9eae-4c97-ae30-36c71b4f13cb]"},{"ResponseStatus": "204"},
{"payara-tracing-parentid": "[0e608033-901d-48c5-8d13-839507128e23]"},
{"host": "[localhost:8080]"},{"content-type": "[application/json]"},
{"connection": "[keep-alive]"},{"user-agent": "[Jersey/2.34.payara-p1
(HttpUrlConnection 11.0.12)]"}]}, {"operationName":"customSpan","spanContext":
{"spanId":"7b3f24a2-1aa3-4b51-af46-019cdd905b3a","traceId":"0e282189-a825-
466e-8488-b2fe569f7a0f"},"startTime":"2021-11-15T18:28:23.206-05:00[America/
New_York]","endTime":"2021-11-15T18:28:23.422066-05:00[America/New_York]",
"traceDuration":"216057000","references":[{"spanContext":{"spanId":"81313a
aa-d744-459c-99c5-aa00e8d679c9","traceId":"0e282189-a825-466e-8488-b2fe
```

569f7a0f"},"relationshipType":"ChildOf"},{"spanContext":{"spanId":"17011bca-7418-42e6-8513-4a586752fb10","traceId":"0e282189-a825-466e-8488-b2fe569f7a0f"},
"relationshipType":"ChildOf"}]},
{"operationName":"PUT:com.ensode.requesttracing.EmployeeResource.hire
Employee","spanContext":{"spanId":"81313aaa-d744-459c-99c5-aa00e8d679c9",
"traceId":"0e282189-a825-466e-8488-b2fe569f7a0f"},"startTime":"2021-11-15T18:
28:23.206-05:00[America/New_York]","endTime":"2021-11-15T18:28:23.428083-05:00
[America/New_York]","traceDuration":"222078000","spanTags":[{"http.status_
code": "204"},{"component": "jaxrs"},{"span.kind": "server"},{"http.url":
"http://localhost:8080/requesttracing/webresources/employeeservice"},{"http.
method": "PUT"}],"references":[{"spanContext":{"spanId":"922671a9-9eae-4c97-
ae30-36c71b4f13cb","traceId":"2f61f32a-c96d-4521-8a82-64e97799f626"},"relati
onshipType":"ChildOf"},{"spanContext":{"spanId":"17011bca-7418-42e6-8513-4a5
86752fb10","traceId":"0e282189-a825-466e-8488-b2fe569f7a0f"},"relation
shipType":"ChildOf"}]}]]

We can add custom tags to our custom spans by invoking setTag(); in the preceding example, we could have added the following line:

```
customSpan.setTag("foo", "bar");
```

to add a tag labeled *foo* with a value of *bar* to our custom span.

## Summary

In this chapter, we covered the request tracing capabilities of Payara Micro. We saw how to enable request tracing via a command-line argument to Payara Micro, which results in all of the RESTful web service endpoints in our application being automatically traced. We also covered how to trace additional methods in our applications via the @Traced annotation, as well as how to disable request tracing in places where it is not desired. Additionally, we covered how to customize the operation name in the spans generated by our applications, as well as how to add custom tags to our spans. Finally, we covered how to programmatically create spans in case we need more control than what is provided by the MicroProfile OpenTracing API.

# CHAPTER 10

# Documenting Web Services

Code documentation is an arduous, often thankless task; for this reason, documentation can easily become obsolete and out of date, as changes are made to the code base; in many occasions, documentation is not updated to reflect the latest changes.

Payara Micro can alleviate this problem via its support for the MicroProfile OpenAPI, which makes generating documentation trivial; in many cases, documentation is updated automatically as the code is updated; for example, adding a new parameter to an existing web service endpoint can result in the new parameter being automatically added to the documentation.

## Automatically Generating Documentation

Any RESTful web service deployed to Payara Micro is automatically documented; to see the generated documentation, all we need to do is send an HTTP GET request to the /openapi endpoint of the Payara Micro instance.

In previous chapters, we've been using a simple human resources system implemented as web services to hire and fire employees; in this chapter, we'll use this same system to illustrate OpenAPI.

The core of the system is a simple RESTful web service that accepts HTTP PUT requests to hire employees and DELETE requests to fire them; as a refresher, here is the source code for our simple RESTful web service:

```
package com.ensode.openapiexample;

//imports omitted
@ApplicationScoped
@Path("employeeservice")
```

© David R. Heffelfinger 2022
D. R. Heffelfinger, *Payara Micro Revealed*, https://doi.org/10.1007/978-1-4842-8161-1_10

```
public class EmployeeResource {

  private List<Employee> employeeList = new CopyOnWriteArrayList<>();
  //thread safe

  @PUT
  @Consumes(MediaType.APPLICATION_JSON)
  public void hireEmployee(Employee employee) {
    employeeList.add(employee);
  }

  @DELETE
  @Consumes(MediaType.APPLICATION_JSON)
  public void fireEmployee(@QueryParam("firstName")
    String firstName, @QueryParam("lastName") String lastName) {

    Optional<Employee> employeeToFire =
      employeeList.stream().filter(emp ->
        emp.getFirstName().equals(firstName) &&
        emp.getLastName().equals(lastName)).findAny();
    employeeToFire.ifPresent(
      emp -> {employeeList.remove(emp);});
  }
}
```

To see the automatically generated documentation for our RESTful web service, we can simply send an HTTP GET request to *http://localhost:8080/openapi* (assuming the project is deployed to our local workstation using the default HTTP port). The easiest way to send the GET request is to point the browser to the preceding URL, as illustrated in Figure 10-1.

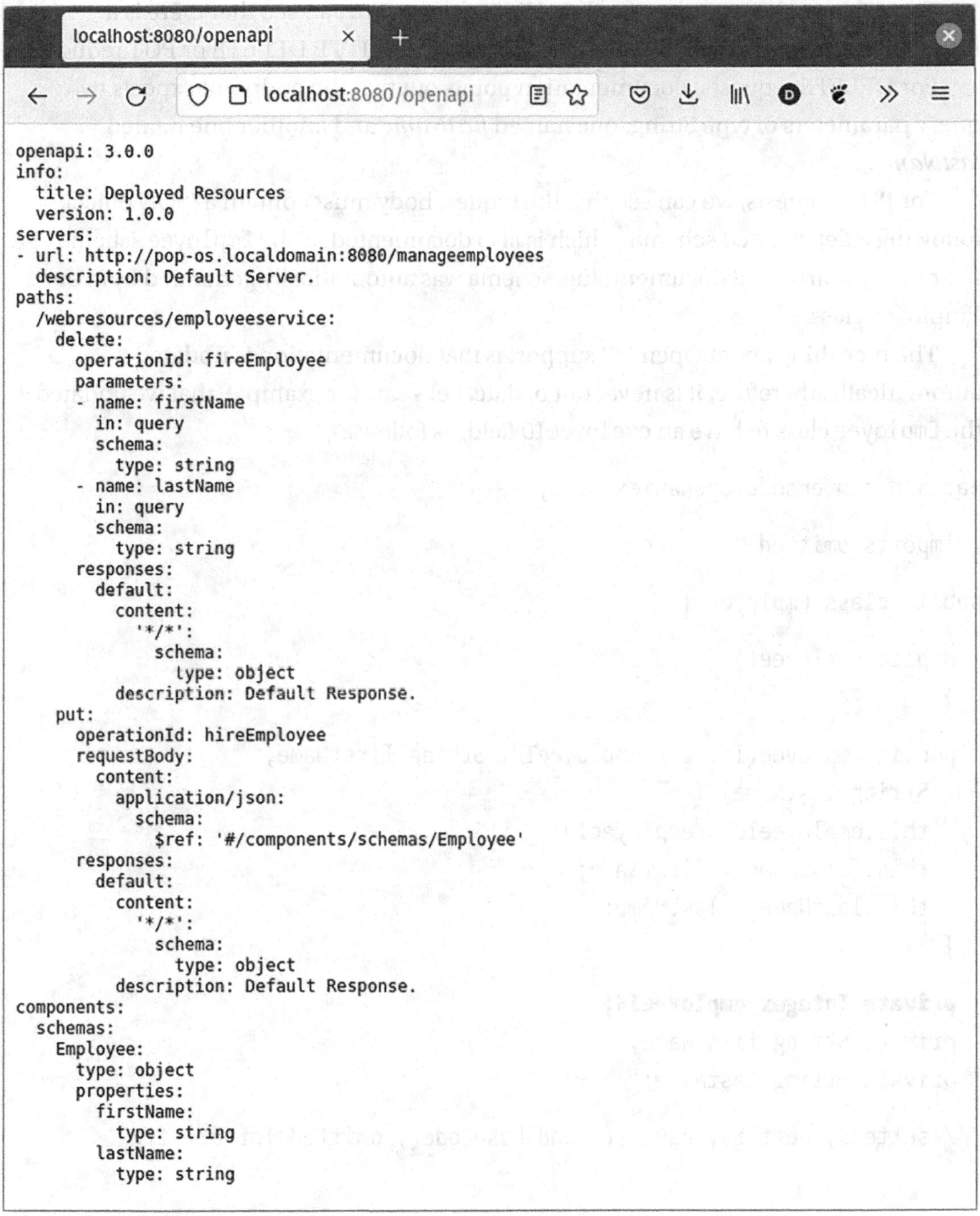

```
openapi: 3.0.0
info:
  title: Deployed Resources
  version: 1.0.0
servers:
- url: http://pop-os.localdomain:8080/manageemployees
  description: Default Server.
paths:
  /webresources/employeeservice:
    delete:
      operationId: fireEmployee
      parameters:
      - name: firstName
        in: query
        schema:
          type: string
      - name: lastName
        in: query
        schema:
          type: string
      responses:
        default:
          content:
            '*/*':
              schema:
                type: object
          description: Default Response.
    put:
      operationId: hireEmployee
      requestBody:
        content:
          application/json:
            schema:
              $ref: '#/components/schemas/Employee'
      responses:
        default:
          content:
            '*/*':
              schema:
                type: object
          description: Default Response.
components:
  schemas:
    Employee:
      type: object
      properties:
        firstName:
          type: string
        lastName:
          type: string
```

***Figure 10-1.*** *Automatically generated documentation*

The generated documentation is in YAML format. We can see that there is a *webresources/employeeservice* path that accepts either HTTP DELETE or PUT requests.

For DELETE requests, documentation points out that the endpoint expects two query parameters of type String: one named *firstName* and another one named *lastName*.

For PUT requests, we can see that the request body must contain a JSON object following a determined schema, which is also documented as the `Employee` schema near the bottom of the document; this schema was automatically generated from our Employee class.

The nice thing about OpenAPI support is that documentation is updated automatically; therefore, it is never out of date. Let's say, for example, that we updated the Employee class to have an `employeeID` field, as follows:

```
package com.ensode.openapiexample;

//imports omitted

public class Employee {

  public Employee() {
  }

  public Employee(Integer employeeId, String firstName,
    String lastName) {
    this.employeeId = employeeId;
    this.firstName = firstName;
    this.lastName = lastName;
  }

  private Integer employeeId;
  private String firstName;
  private String lastName;

  //setters, getters, equals() and hashCode() omitted for brevity

}
```

Suppose then we updated the `fireEmployee()` method to accept `employeeID` as a query parameter:

```
package com.ensode.openapiexample;

//imports omitted

@ApplicationScoped
@Path("employeeservice")
public class EmployeeResource {

  private List<Employee> employeeList = new CopyOnWriteArrayList<>();
  //thread safe

  @PUT
  @Consumes(MediaType.APPLICATION_JSON)
  public void hireEmployee(Employee employee) {
    employeeList.add(employee);
  }

  @DELETE
  @Consumes(MediaType.APPLICATION_JSON)
  public void fireEmployee(
    @QueryParam("employeeId") Integer employeeID) {

    Optional<Employee> employeeToFire =
      employeeList.stream().filter(emp →
      emp.getEmployeeId().equals(employeeID)).findAny();
    employeeToFire.ifPresent(
      emp -> {
        employeeList.remove(emp);
      });
  }
}
```

After deploying our application, we point our browser to *http://localhost:8080/ openapi* again and see that our documentation has been updated automatically, with zero effort on our part.

Notice that in the documentation, *operationID fireEmployee* now takes a single parameter named *employeeID*, and near the bottom of the document, the *Employee* schema has been automatically updated to have an additional *employeeID* property of type integer; all of these updates were driven directly by our code changes, no need for us to even think about updating the documentation. We can see the updated documentation in Figure 10-2.

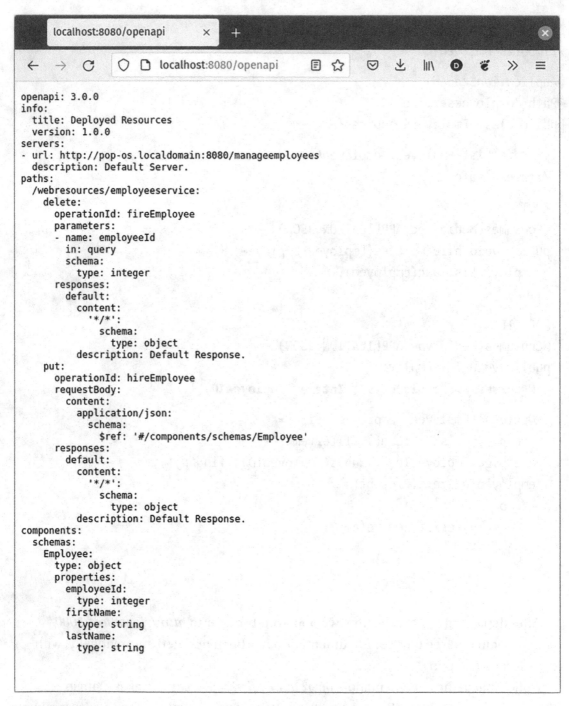

```
openapi: 3.0.0
info:
  title: Deployed Resources
  version: 1.0.0
servers:
- url: http://pop-os.localdomain:8080/manageemployees
  description: Default Server.
paths:
  /webresources/employeeservice:
    delete:
      operationId: fireEmployee
      parameters:
      - name: employeeId
        in: query
        schema:
          type: integer
      responses:
        default:
          content:
            '*/*':
              schema:
                type: object
          description: Default Response.
    put:
      operationId: hireEmployee
      requestBody:
        content:
          application/json:
            schema:
              $ref: '#/components/schemas/Employee'
      responses:
        default:
          content:
            '*/*':
              schema:
                type: object
          description: Default Response.
components:
  schemas:
    Employee:
      type: object
      properties:
        employeeId:
          type: integer
        firstName:
          type: string
        lastName:
          type: string
```

***Figure 10-2.***  *Automatically updated documentation*

As previously mentioned, by default, documentation is generated in YAML format; if we want to generate in JSON instead, we can do it by passing a query parameter named *format* with a value of *json* to the */openapi* endpoint, for example:

```
http://localhost:8080/openapi?format=json
```

Figure 10-3 illustrates the equivalent documentation for our updated service, this time in JSON format.

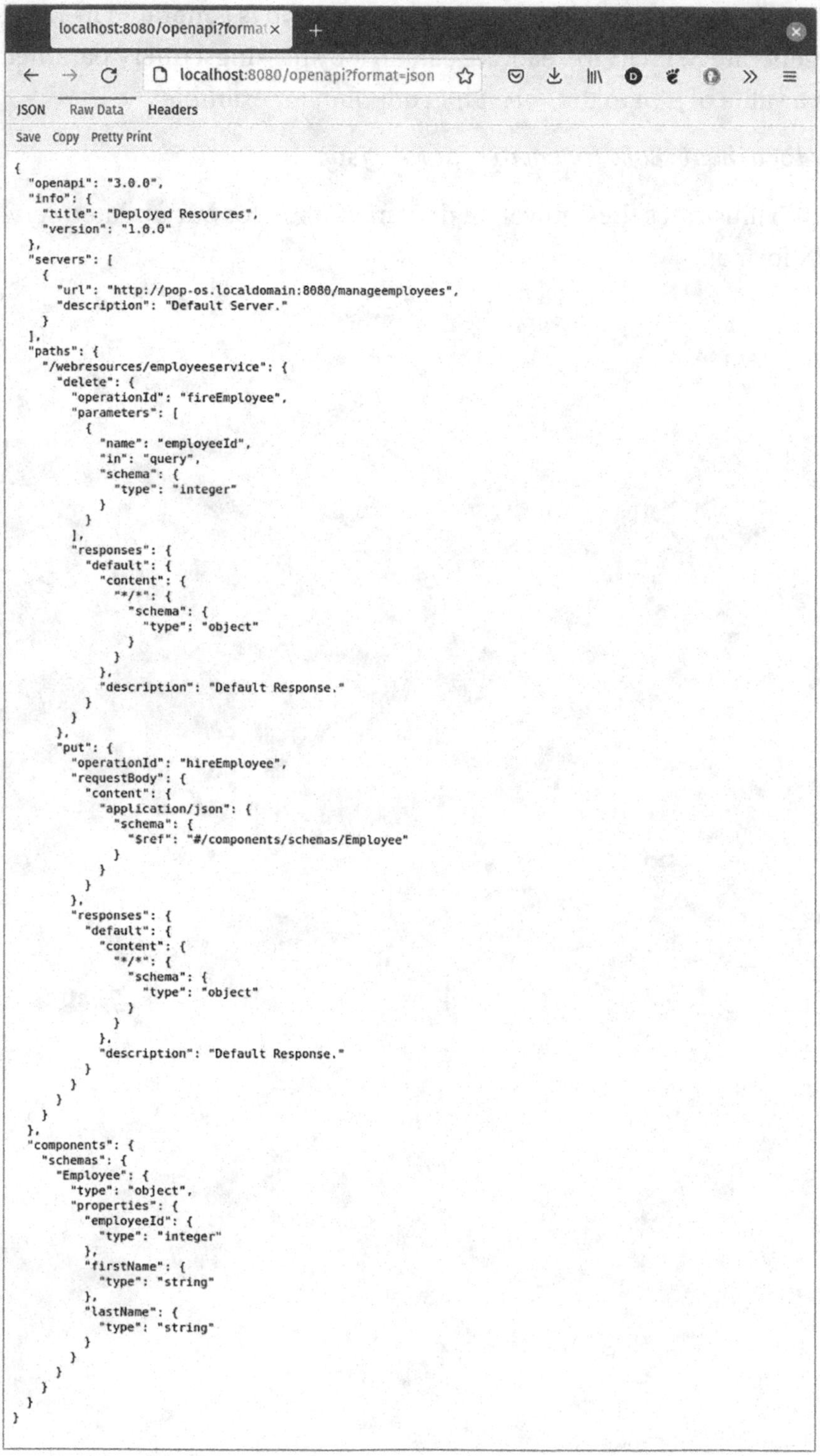
localhost:8080/openapi?format
localhost:8080/openapi?format=json
JSON
Raw Data
Headers
Save
Copy
Pretty Print
{
  "openapi": "3.0.0",
  "info": {
    "title": "Deployed Resources",
    "version": "1.0.0"
  },
  "servers": [
    {
      "url": "http://pop-os.localdomain:8080/manageemployees",
      "description": "Default Server."
    }
  ],
  "paths": {
    "/webresources/employeeservice": {
      "delete": {
        "operationId": "fireEmployee",
        "parameters": [
          {
            "name": "employeeId",
            "in": "query",
            "schema": {
              "type": "integer"
            }
          }
        ],
        "responses": {
          "default": {
            "content": {
              "*/*": {
                "schema": {
                  "type": "object"
                }
              }
            },
            "description": "Default Response."
          }
        }
      },
      "put": {
        "operationId": "hireEmployee",
        "requestBody": {
          "content": {
            "application/json": {
              "schema": {
                "$ref": "#/components/schemas/Employee"
              }
            }
          }
        },
        "responses": {
          "default": {
            "content": {
              "*/*": {
                "schema": {
                  "type": "object"
                }
              }
            },
            "description": "Default Response."
          }
        }
      }
    }
  },
  "components": {
    "schemas": {
      "Employee": {
        "type": "object",
        "properties": {
          "employeeId": {
            "type": "integer"
          },
          "firstName": {
            "type": "string"
          },
          "lastName": {
            "type": "string"
          }
        }
      }
    }
  }
}

***Figure 10-3.*** *Automatically updated documentation, in JSON format*

# Customizing Documentation via Code Annotations

OpenAPI provides annotations we can use to customize the generated documentation.

## Customizing HTTP Responses

We can customize the generated documentation for the response; we can additionally add descriptions for different HTTP codes returned by our endpoint; this can be achieved by annotating methods in our Jakarta RESTful web services with the @APIResponse annotation.

Suppose we added an endpoint to our human resources application to find an employee by ID; upon successfully finding an employee, an HTTP code of 200 ("OK") is automatically returned; if we don't find the employee, we can trigger an HTTP code of 404 ("not found") by throwing a NotFoundException. We could document this behavior in the code by using the @APIResponse annotation.

```
@GET
@APIResponse(responseCode = "200",
  description = "Employee found",
  content = @Content(mediaType = APPLICATION_JSON,
                     schema =
                     @Schema(implementation = Employee.class))
@APIResponse(responseCode = "404",
        description = "Employee not found ")
public Employee findEmployee(
  @QueryParam("employeeId") Integer employeeID) {
  Optional<Employee> employeeToFind =
    employeeList.stream().filter(emp →
    emp.getEmployeeId().equals(employeeID)).findFirst();

    return employeeToFind.orElseThrow(
      () -> new NotFoundException()); //if not found, return a 404
}
```

As we can see from the preceding example, @APIResponse has three attributes; responseCode and description are self-explanatory; the optional content attribute designates the media type and schema of the response body, if any.

181

Figure 10-4 illustrates the relevant parts of the updated documentation for our application.

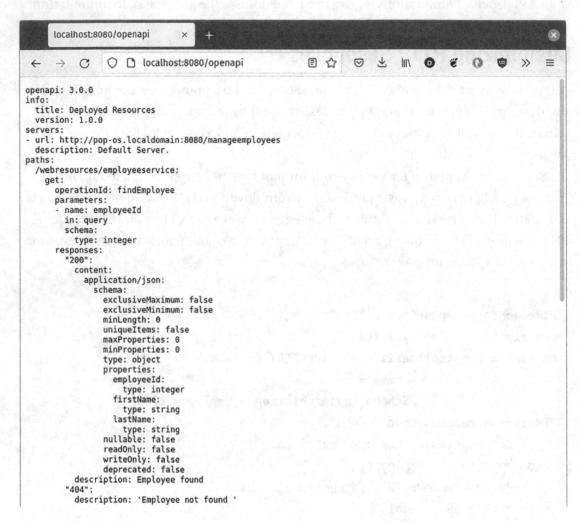

***Figure 10-4.*** *Documentation generated by the @APIResponse annotation*

Our new method was automatically added, with no additional effort on our part; notice the descriptions for HTTP codes 200 and 404 for *operationId findEmployee* (our new method); those were generated by the @APIResponse annotations we added to the method.

# Customizing Documentation for Operations

By default, each endpoint on our RESTful web services is given an operation ID matching its method name; this is how the *operationID* fields for the documentation on how the endpoint responds to HTTP GET, PUT, and DELETE requests were generated in our example.

If we want to override the generated operationID, we can do so with the @Operation annotation; this annotation also allows us to provide summary and detailed descriptions of our operations, as illustrated in the following example:

```
@GET
@Operation(operationId = "Find Employee",
  summary = "Finds an employee",
  description = "Finds an employee from the given employee ID, returns an
HTTP code 404 if the employee is not found")
@APIResponse(responseCode = "200",
  description = "Employee found",
  content = @Content(mediaType = APPLICATION_JSON, schema =
    @Schema(implementation = Employee.class)))
@APIResponse(responseCode = "404",
  description = "Employee not found ")
public Employee findEmployee(@QueryParam("employeeId") Integer
employeeID) {
  Optional<Employee> employeeToFind =
    employeeList.stream().filter(emp →
    emp.getEmployeeId().equals(employeeID)).findFirst();

  return employeeToFind.orElseThrow(
    () -> new NotFoundException());
}
```

The operationID attribute of the @Operation annotation overrides the generated *operationId* in the documentation. The summary and description attributes provide brief and detailed descriptions of the operation, respectively.

Figure 10-5 illustrates the updated documentation for the operation.

**Figure 10-5.** *Custom operation ID*

Notice the updated *operationID*, as well as the new *summary* and *description* fields that were generated as a result of the @Operation annotation.

## Customizing Documentation for Path or Query Parameters

Path or query parameters are annotated with @PathParam or @QueryParam. OpenAPI generates default documentation for either parameter type; if we wish, we can add additional information about our parameters to the generated documentation; we can do this via the @Parameter annotation, as illustrated in the following example:

```
@GET
@Operation(operationId = "Find Employee",
  summary = "Finds an employee",
  description = "Finds an employee from the given employee ID, returns an
HTTP code 404 if the employee is not found")
@APIResponse(responseCode = "200",
  description = "Employee found",
  content = @Content(mediaType = APPLICATION_JSON, schema =
    @Schema(implementation = Employee.class)))
@APIResponse(responseCode = "404",
  description = "Employee not found ")
public Employee findEmployee(@QueryParam("employeeId")
  @Parameter(description = "Employee ID", required = true)
  Integer employeeID) {
  Optional<Employee> employeeToFind =
    employeeList.stream().filter(emp →
    emp.getEmployeeId().equals(employeeID)).findFirst();

  return employeeToFind.orElseThrow(
    () -> new NotFoundException());
  }
```

In this example, we are adding a description to our employeeID query parameter, as well as specifying that the parameter is required. Figure 10-6 illustrates the relevant parts of the updated documentation.

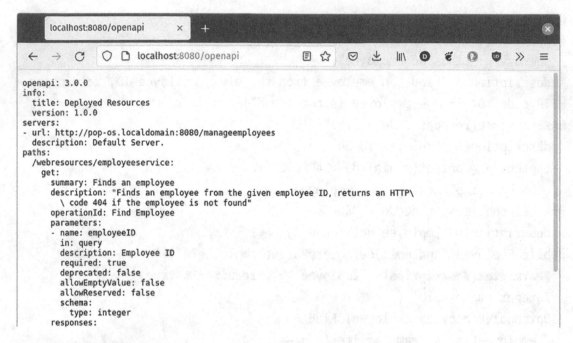

*Figure 10-6.* *Custom parameter documentation*

Notice that the *employeeID* parameter in the documentation now has a description and is documented as being required, both as a result of the @Parameter annotation added to our query parameter.

# Configuring OpenAPI

OpenAPI can be configured via the MicroProfile Config API via standard configuration properties that must be supported by every MicroProfile implementation. Additionally, Payara Micro provides additional configuration options via pre or post boot command files.

## Configuring OpenAPI via MicroProfile Config

OpenAPI provides a number of properties that can be used to customize its behavior; these properties can be set in any source supported by MicroProfile Config (*microprofile-config.properties*, environment variables, system properties, etc.).

Table 10-1 summarizes all properties that can be used to customize OpenAPI.

***Table 10-1.***  *OpenAPI MicroProfile Config Properties*

| Property | Description |
|---|---|
| mp.openapi.model.reader | Fully qualified name of an implementation of the OASModelReader interface, which can be used to programmatically create or augment the documentation |
| mp.openapi.filter | Fully qualified name of an implementation of the OASFilter interface, which can be used to implement callbacks to be executed when OpenAPI annotations are processed |
| mp.openapi.scan.disable | Used to disable documentation generation |
| mp.openapi.scan.packages | Used to specify which packages to scan when procession OpenAPI annotations |
| mp.openapi.scan.classes | Used to specify which classes to scan when processing OpenAPI annotations |
| mp.openapi.scan.exclude. packages | Used to specify which packages to exclude when processing OpenAPI annotations |
| mp.openapi.scan.exclude. classes | Used to specify which classes to exclude when processing OpenAPI annotations |
| mp.openapi.scan.lib | Used to specify If classes in JAR files inside the WAR file should be scanned for OpenAPI annotations |
| mp.openapi.servers | Used to specify a list of global servers that provide connectivity information |
| mp.openapi.servers.path. | Prefix of a property used to specify an alternative list of servers to service all operations in a path. For example, mp.openapi.servers. path./employeemanagement=https://example.com/v1 |
| mp.openapi.servers. operation. | Prefix of a property used to specify an alternative list of servers to service an operation. The remainder of the property name must be the operationId of the endpoint in question. For example, mp.openapi.servers.operation.hireEmployee=https:// example.com/v1 |
| mp.openapi.schema. | Prefix of a property to specify a schema for a specific Java class, in JSON format. The remainder of the property name must be a fully qualified Java class name. The value must be a valid OpenAPI schema object, specified in JSON format |

# Configuring OpenAPI via a Payara Micro Command File

We can configure OpenAPI in Payara Micro via the `set-openapi-configuration` asadmin command via a command file passed as a post boot command file or similar.

## Disabling OpenAPI

Payara Micro enables OpenAPI by default; if we wish to disable it, we can use the following asadmin command:

```
set-openapi-configuration --enabled=false
```

## Enabling CORS Headers

Cross-Origin Resource Sharing (CORS) headers can be added to OpenAPI endpoint responses by issuing the following asadmin command:

```
set-openapi-configuration --corsheaders=true
```

## Securing OpenAPI

By default, the *openapi* endpoint is unsecured, meaning any random unauthenticated user can access it.

If we wish to secure it, we can do so by issuing the following asadmin command:

```
set-openapi-configuration --securityenabled=true
```

When securing the *openapi* endpoint, we can specify which roles have access to it as follows:

```
set-openapi-configuration --roles=role1,role2
```

The value of the `--roles` argument is a comma-separated list of roles allowed to access the health endpoint.

## Customizing the OpenAPI Endpoint

By default, documentation can be retrieved via the *openapi* endpoint. We can use a different endpoint if we wish.

```
set-openapi-configuration --endpoint=foo
```

The value of the *--endpoint* argument is the context root of our custom OpenAPI endpoint.

# Summary

In this chapter, we covered how documentation for our RESTful web services is generated automatically from JAX-RS annotations, resulting in documentation that is never out of date with the code.

Then we covered how to use OpenAPI annotations to customize the generated documentation.

Lastly, we covered how to configure OpenAPI via MicroProfile Config and via asadmin commands.

# CHAPTER 11

# Security with JSON Web Tokens

Traditionally, security in web applications has been implemented by keeping data about the logged-in user in the HTTP session. With microservices being inherently stateless, this approach is not suitable for a microservices architecture. To address security, MicroProfile has support for JSON Web Token (JWT).

JSON Web Tokens are a mechanism used to implement stateless security in microservices.

JWT is a JSON-based text format used for exchanging information between systems. JWT is an open standard, specified under RFC 7519. A JWT's information is encapsulated in *claims,* which are essentially key value pairs. MicroProfile requires JWTs to be digitally signed using the RSA-SHA256 algorithm.

JWTs can contain arbitrary claims, all of them optional; the MicroProfile JWT specification, though, requires specific claims.

| JWT Claim | Description |
|-----------|-------------|
| iss | Token issuer |
| at | The time the token was issued, it is specified as a long value representing the number of seconds between January 1, 1970 UTC and the issued time |
| exp | The time the token will expire, it is specified as a long value representing the number of seconds between January 1, 1970 UTC and the expiration time |
| upn | The username of the logged-in principal |

© David R. Heffelfinger 2022
D. R. Heffelfinger, *Payara Micro Revealed*, https://doi.org/10.1007/978-1-4842-8161-1_11

In addition to the required claims, the MicroProfile JWT specification recommends the following claims to be present in a JWT:

| JWT Claim | Description |
| --- | --- |
| jti | Unique identifier for the JWT |
| aud | Identifies the recipients that the JWT is intended for, interpretation of audience values is application specific |
| groups | Any security groups (AKA roles) that the user belongs to |

# Obtaining a Token

A JWT is typically obtained from some sort of identity server; when deploying to the cloud, most cloud providers provide a way to obtain a JWT to use with their servers. If deploying applications in-house, a JWT is typically obtained by an identity server tool deployed in-house, for example, something like the open source Keycloak tool or through commercial identity servers such as Okta or similar.

For testing and learning purposes, these tools are a bit overkill; thankfully, there is an open source tool developed by the prolific Java consultant Adam Bien, the tool is called *jwtenizr*, we can use it to quickly and easily generate a JWT for testing purposes.

jwtenizr can be downloaded from *http://jwtenizr.sh/*; it is a self-contained, executable JAR file; we can generate a token by issuing the following command from the command line:

```
java -jar jwtenizr.jar
```

The preceding command will generate output similar to the following:

```
Enable verbose output with java -Dverbose -jar jwtenizr.jar [optional: an
URI for the generated curl]
The generated token token.jwt contains information loaded from:
jwt-token.json
Adjust the groups[] to configure roles and upn to change the principal in
jwt-token.json then re-execute JWTenizr
The iss in jwt-token.json has to correspond with the mp.jwt.verify.issuer
in microprofile-config.properties
```

Copy the `microprofile-config.properties` to your WAR/src/main/resources/
META-INF

Use the following command for testing:

```
curl -i -H'Authorization: Bearer eyJraWQiOiJqd3Qua2V5IiwidHlwIjoiSldUIiwi
YWxnIjoiUlMyNTYifQ.eyJzdWIiOiJkdWtlIiwidXBuIjoiZHVrZSIsImF1dGhfdGltZSI6MTY
zOTQwODk4NywiaXNzIjoiYWlyaGFja3MiLCJncm91cHMiOlsiY2hpZWYiLCJoYWNrZXIiXS
wiZXhwIjoxNjM5NDA5OTg3LCJpYXQiOjE2Mzk0MDg5ODcsImp0aSI6IjQyIn0.
GnSwzNSO7EfKRD-ANqYhaVQuY8HIRdp29r-8K3lqpjCb2bByRmkdqTl9HPW4ePfqeOK7wpr_1Nf
ir12CPSb9e4i1PWw-qZxf9pPpEIeLRVB-_8p_n6FaTCkt4uSB12fcBMaLh2PZGOAnK5uWjAY1V-
noD-KxmX_BsZnhSOssMa-OFnmevXlYPcRcbauVUxlTOACzFwdxpcRSq_Ms9QMh_5TctQZtq59VT
npOnfOZBIHd3eSOzB6AHqqNNtioPW8syX6iZxweSQkBXOpmYBaQxC2iUExhUOTmzEnDeBjaJ5Ec
dvAZO-98w2GIqnZrftBlQvtWt25MKmNIl_NAtmBKZQ' http://localhost:8080
```

`[10:23:07:548]JWT generated`

Notice that the output of the tool includes example usage on how to invoke secured services using *curl*, very handy when testing our services.

jwtenizr generates a number of files:

- jwtenizr-config.json: A JSON file we can use to configure jwtenizr, can be used to customize the JWT issuer and the location of the generated sample MicroProfile configuration file; it will be read in subsequent executions of jwtenizr.

- jwt-token.json: Cleartext version of the generated JWT.

- microprofile-config.properties: Sample microprofile-config. properties we can use to configure our secured applications.

- token.jwt: Base 64 encoded version of the generated JWT.

Although JWT is fairly configurable, its defaults will suffice for our purposes. By default, jwtenizr generates a token for a user called "duke", belonging to groups "chief" and "hacker", issued by "airhacks", and expiring 16 minutes and 40 seconds (1,000 seconds) from the time the token was created.

# Securing Microservices with JSON Web Tokens

Securing our RESTful web services is primarily done via a few simple MicroProfile Config properties and some annotations.

## MicroProfile Config JWT Properties

As previously mentioned, JSON Web Tokens are digitally signed; this is done by encrypting the token with the issuer's private key. To verify the validity of the token, we need to decrypt it with the issuer's public key.

MicroProfile JWT provides a standard configuration property we can use to specify the public key; the name of the property is `mp.jwt.verify.publickey`; its value must be the Base 64 encoded public key; this value is typically provided by whichever identity service we may be using. In our example, the value appears in the sample MicroProfile configuration file generated by jwtenizr.

Alternatively, we could put the public key in a text file and either publish that text file in a URL or place it inside the JAR file; in a typical Maven project, the file containing the public key would be placed under *src/main/resources* or one of its subdirectories.

If, for example, we placed the key under *src/main/resources/keys/publicKey.pem*, the value of the `mp.jwt.verify.publickey` property would be `/keys/publicKey.pem`; if, instead, we placed the public key directly in *src/main/resources*, then the corresponding property value would be `/publicKey.pem`.

In addition to specifying the public key, we need to specify the issuer of the token; this is specified in the *iss* claim of the JWT we are using and can be obtained from the cleartext JSON Web Token we are using to authenticate. jwtenizr uses *airhacks* as its default issuer; therefore, we must configure our application accordingly. jwtenizr conveniently generates a `microprofile-config.properties` we can use; it should look similar to the following:

```
#generated by jwtenizr
#Mon Dec 13 18:05:17 EST 2021
mp.jwt.verify.publickey=MIIBIjANBgkqhkiG9w0BAQEFAAOCAQ8AMIIBCgKCAQEArO
mNhZNAb2UXrMQ+TOp4hOCX4/QN1lC7DJW9Sw8PRZF85SrxKe2rAt8uOaaPg8KZdYsmAfxJU7Zs
ILHFV7cT9ixYyZcIz556CpluhQmJiVlBEDi6lX9IIbhXsfeaCXPATd+OfeOYg4CLtfGeJj
ZQQOK8yabqsRemhQ84s/alCfWeWm7zpODHeOPH+2kNkLVeSg4cigAzakDiW9JYNs5+7XzqPujY
```

pNOjJqCltDfPkzOcObqIOMKr7cmOG+WTQIqXxI46y1vUTYCdH+irJuJF8FPlL84Rd1NY
rRtCLslFhqfLhSELYRWu7lyXsH89QSAjFTmY1ofzmWdawPYkIIQJrwIDAQAB
mp.jwt.verify.issuer=airhacks

Placing the file under *src/main/resources/META-INF* in our Maven project will take care of our JWT configuration needs.

## MicroProfile JWT Annotations

Every JAX-RS application requires an instance of a class that extends `javax.ws.rs.core.Application`; typically, we annotate this class with `@ApplicationPath` to specify the base URI for all resource URIs in our application. When securing our applications, we need to annotate this class with the `@LoginConfig` annotation as illustrated in the following example.

```
package com.ensode.jwtdemo;

import javax.inject.Singleton;
import javax.ws.rs.ApplicationPath;
import javax.ws.rs.core.Application;
import org.eclipse.microprofile.auth.LoginConfig;

@Singleton
@ApplicationPath("webresources")
@LoginConfig(authMethod = "MP-JWT")
public class ApplicationConfig extends Application {

}
```

As seen in the example, we need to set the `authMethod` attribute of `@LoginConfig` to `"MP-JWT"`; this tells the MicroProfile runtime (Payara Micro) that our application is using JWT for authentication.

Additionally, our application class needs to be turned into a singleton by annotating it with `javax.inject.Singleton`; failure to do this will prevent clients from being authenticated properly.

Once we have specified we are using JWT for authentication, we need to specify which roles can access our protected endpoints; this is done via the `@RolesAllowed` annotation, as illustrated in the following example:

```
package com.ensode.jwtdemo;

import javax.annotation.security.RolesAllowed;
//additional imports omitted

@RequestScoped
@Path("jwtdemo")
public class JwtDemoResource {

  @GET
  @Produces(MediaType.TEXT_PLAIN)
  @RolesAllowed({"chief"})
  public String secured() {
    return "Secured endpoint accessed successfully\n";
  }
}
```

The @RolesAllowed annotation can be used at the class level, in which case it will apply to all endpoints in the class, or at the method level, in which case it will only apply to the annotated method; its value must be an array of strings containing valid roles that are allowed to access the endpoint; these roles are taken from the *groups* claim in the JWT. In our example, we used jwtenizr to generate our token, which, by default, creates a token with the following groups/roles: "chief" and "hacker"; in our example, only users with the role of "chief" will be able to access the endpoint.

In order for the @RolesAllowed annotation to work as expected, we need to turn our JAX-RS class into a CDI request scoped bean via the @RequestScoped annotation, as illustrated in the example.

We can test our secured endpoint with curl by sending the Base 64 encoded token as an HTTP header, for example:

```
curl -H'Authorization: Bearer eyJraWQiOiJqd3Qua2V5IiwidHlwIjoiSldUIiwiYWxn
IjoiUlMyNTYifQ.eyJzdWIiOiJkdWtlIiwidXBuIjoiZHVrZSIsImF1dGhfdGltZSI6MTYzOTQ
zOTIxNCwiaXNzIjoiYWlyaGFja3MiLCJncm91cHMiOlsiY2hpZWYiLCJoYWNrZXIiXSwiZX
hwIjoxNjM5NDQwMjEwLCJpYXQiOjE2MzkOMzkyMTQsImp0aSI6IjQyIn0.gMwd042R8L_
pxmj97j9Bzsz8Vg5cZCSZ_uiSJwqnBD5i811Wq_4l9_DQ-LdRGQwgORKrN3emVfkxOiiWn
TSSfEIOKDktuCiJuhlcojeaTvpACaFtnYLI5fZ6hCkurj7TEnrJwVqxJVo_dH6AS45UR2Q
3z688oBBSb5_i5gtw9g_84nkWp7OFkAjDusz-jLWeebOWAEk6NRv6fN_ZAP1JJcz9WoNord
```

MeXgVe2tFmLz8_yDY_ba-Ox1F9vEXBalHz4AwJaAYtW97mvshdnLnKkP48mQGoO4X9Ps6eRCG1
viTuTmcHRTACt9osb7wssWIDenhuumz_lI9P9sLVFfj29Q' http://localhost:8080/jwt-
demo/webresources/jwtdemo

The preceding *curl* command will result in a successful invocation to our endpoint;
if we remove the -H option from the command, then the request will fail with an HTTP
status code of 401: Unauthorized.

To authorize requests via the MicroProfile REST client API, we need to send the Base
64 encoded token as well; we will cover how to do this in the next section.

# Invoking Secured Microservices with MicroProfile REST Client API

In order to invoke a secured RESTful web service via the MicroProfile REST client API,
we need to write an interface, and it needs to be annotated with @RegisterRestClient
as usual; however, in this case, there are some slight differences in the method signature
and annotations used in the client interface, compared to the code implementing the
endpoint.

```
package com.ensode.jwtclientdemo;

import javax.ws.rs.HeaderParam;
import javax.ws.rs.core.HttpHeaders;
//other imports omitted

@RegisterRestClient
@Path("jwtdemo")
public interface JwtDemoResourceClient {

  @GET
  @Produces(MediaType.TEXT_PLAIN)
  public String secured(@HeaderParam(HttpHeaders.AUTHORIZATION)
    String authorizationHeader);
}
```

The first thing to note is that we should not use the @RolesAllowed annotation on the client interface; this would result in the client itself being secured, which is not what we want in our example; what we are aiming to do here is to invoke a secured endpoint from an unsecured one; in order to do that, we need to send the JWT token as an HTTP header.

We can send an HTTP header in by annotating a String parameter with the @HeaderParam annotation; the value attribute of this annotation specifies the header name; since "Authorization" is a standard HTTP header name, it is defined as the AUTHORIZATION constant in the HttpHeaders class.

---

Notice that the method signature does not exactly match the corresponding signature in the JAX-RS service code; the endpoint does not define the authorizationHeader parameter.

---

We use the REST client interface as usual by injecting it via the @Inject and @RestClient annotations and then passing the JWT token as a parameter that will be processed as an HTTP header, thanks to the @HeaderParam interface.

```
package com.ensode.jwtclientdemo;

//imports omitted

@ApplicationScoped
@Path("jwtclient")
public class JwtClientResource {

  @Inject
  @RestClient
  private JwtDemoResourceClient jwtDemoResourceClient;

  @Inject
  @ConfigProperty(name = "ensode.jwt.header.string")
  private String jwtHeaderString;
```

```
@GET
public String accessSecuredEndpoint() {
  jwtDemoResourceClient.secured(
    "Bearer ".concat(jwtHeaderString));
  return "secured endpoint accessed successfully";
  }
}
```

We can obtain the JWT token as a simple string; in our example, we are setting it up as a MicroProfile Config property and retrieving it from there; we then invoke the client method, passing the JWT token as a parameter; in order for authentication to work as expected, we need to prefix the token text with the word "Bearer", which we are doing as we invoke the method on the client interface.

For completeness and clarity, here is the property file we used to store the JWT text:

com.ensode.jwtclientdemo.JwtDemoResourceClient/mp-rest/url=http://
localhost:8080/jwt-demo/webresources
ensode.jwt.header.string=eyJraWQiOiJqd3Qua2V5IiwidHlwIjoiSldUIiwiYWxnIjoi
UlMyNTYifQ.eyJzdWIiOiJkdWtlIiwidXBuIjoiZHVrZSIsImF1dGhfdGltZSI6MTYzOTQ4ODc
40CwiaXNzIjoiYWlyaGFja3MiLCJncm91cHMiOlsiY2hpZWYiLCJoYWNrZXIiXSwiZXhwIjox
NjM5NDg5Nzg4LCJpYXQiOjE2Mzk0ODg3ODgsImp0aSI6IjQyIn0.C9_ejgLALOo8IVHZ6P6fqo
TrVIjrmaqJ_gexHrEzwxOjWExDwLmKLIWKcOHWytKPrWOk1ok8cKUj55rKWG8Vp1-gGhIp
tWeGF2ckSKu5fCOaoBerJn6x8uDJVeURV8-ABHcoJFSePQx3EEGmoLEb2_EqgBvU4didp-
MyUwyyIKiDIuOSu_n-mFq_yB9WpZZiY4lyNS9ewt_TDUmIgteJ2VMsmZaHp3n_RygVOS4FPXhOU
HRhKOfLLUorvJzGYsT7dgjbnY6kyh4dgAXWrGnX4kafOZFyVXCxsmuvks9Ixltv6krqWe_j-OZ
kYMzevgnXbvc3MA9LJWQMhauwtGfw1g

Notice how the JWT token text is specified as the value of the ensode.jwt.header. string property, which we retrieve in our code via the @ConfigProperty annotation and pass to the client interface.

# Obtaining Information from a Token

We can inject an instance of org.eclipse.microprofile.jwt.JsonWebToken into
our JAX-RS resource; this class has a number of getter methods we can use to extract
information from the token that was used to access the page.

```java
package com.ensode.jwtdemo;

//additional imports omitted
import org.eclipse.microprofile.jwt.JsonWebToken;

@RequestScoped
@Path("jwtdemo")
public class JwtDemoResource {

  private static final Logger LOGGER = Logger.getLogger(JwtDemoResource.
  class.getName());

  @Inject
  private JsonWebToken jsonWebToken;

  @GET
  @Produces(MediaType.TEXT_PLAIN)
  @RolesAllowed({"chief"})
  public String secured() {

    LOGGER.log(Level.INFO, String.format("Audience: %s",
      jsonWebToken.getAudience()));
    LOGGER.log(Level.INFO, String.format("Expiration Time: %s",
      jsonWebToken.getExpirationTime()));
    LOGGER.log(Level.INFO, String.format("Groups: %s",
      jsonWebToken.getGroups()));
    LOGGER.log(Level.INFO, String.format("Issued at time: %s",
      jsonWebToken.getIssuedAtTime()));
    LOGGER.log(Level.INFO, String.format("Issuer: %s",
      jsonWebToken.getIssuer()));
    LOGGER.log(Level.INFO, String.format("Name: %s",
      jsonWebToken.getName()));
```

```
    LOGGER.log(Level.INFO, String.format("Raw Token: %s",
      jsonWebToken.getRawToken()));
    LOGGER.log(Level.INFO, String.format("Subject: %s",
     jsonWebToken.getSubject()));
    LOGGER.log(Level.INFO, String.format("Token ID: %s",
      jsonWebToken.getTokenID()));

    return "Secured endpoint accessed successfully\n";
  }
}
```

The following table lists all the getter methods we can use to extract information from the token, along with the corresponding claim where the information is extracted from.

| Getter Method | JWT Claim | Description |
| --- | --- | --- |
| getAudience() | aud | Intended audience |
| getExpirationTime() | exp | Expiration time, as the number of seconds since January 1, 1970 UTC |
| getGroups() | groups | The groups (or roles) the user belongs to |
| getIssuedAtTime() | iat | The time the token was issued, expiration time, as the number of seconds since January 1, 1970 UTC |
| getIssuer() | iss | Organization that issued the token |
| getName() | upn | Unique Principal Name (the username) |
| getRawToken() | N/A | Base 64 encoded string representing the token (the value that we pass as the HTTP authorization header) |
| getSubject() | sub | Additional identifier for the user could be used to store the user's full name (i.e., "John Doe") |
| getTokenId() | jti | JSON Token ID |

All of the preceding getter methods are for claims that the MicroProfile JWT specification either requires or recommends; if any of the recommended claims is not present, the getter will return null. A JWT token, though, may have an arbitrary number of claims, many of which we don't have a getter method for.

If we know in advance the name of a claim whose value we would like to retrieve, we can do so by invoking the `claim()` method on an instance of `JsonWebToken`; for example, if we know our token has a claim named "foo", we can obtain its value by invoking `jsonWebToken.claim("foo")`.

There may be times when we don't know in advance all the claim names in our token; to handle this situation, the `JsonWebToken` class has a `claimNames()` method that returns a set of strings containing all the claim names in our token; we can use this set to obtain the values of all claims in our token; the following example illustrates how to do this:

```
package com.ensode.jwtdemo;

//imports omitted

@RequestScoped
@Path("jwtdemo")
public class JwtDemoResource {

  private static final Logger LOGGER = Logger.getLogger(JwtDemoResource.
  class.getName());

  @Inject
  private JsonWebToken jsonWebToken;

  @GET
  @Produces(MediaType.TEXT_PLAIN)
  @RolesAllowed({"chief"})
  public String secured() {

    Set<String> claimNames = jsonWebToken.getClaimNames();

    LOGGER.log(Level.INFO, "--- Begin Token Claims");
    claimNames.forEach(claimName -> LOGGER.log(Level.INFO,
            String.format("%s: %s", claimName,
                    jsonWebToken.claim(claimName).orElse(""))));
    LOGGER.log(Level.INFO, "--- End Token Claims");

    return "Secured endpoint accessed successfully\n";
  }
}
```

In this example, we obtain a `Set` of `String` containing all the claim names, then traverse the set and extract the value of each claim, and then send the output to the Payara Micro output. Recall that `JsonWebToken.claim()` returns an `Optional`; in our example, if the `Optional` happens to be empty, use an empty `String` (`""`) as the corresponding value.

# Summary

In this chapter, we covered how to secure our RESTful web services with JSON Web Tokens.

We covered how to obtain a token so that we can use it to secure our applications; we then explained how to configure our RESTful web services so that they require authentication.

Additionally, we covered how to securely invoke a secured RESTful web service.

Finally, we covered how to extract information from a JSON Web Token in our code.

# Payara Micro Specific Features

In previous chapters, we've been focusing primarily on Payara Micro's implementation of the MicroProfile standard. The benefit of coding against a standard is that we are not tied to a specific implementation, as code written against the standard can be deployed to any implementation.

In this chapter, we will cover some Payara Micro specific features that, while very useful, are specific to Payara Micro and not portable across implementations.

## Automatic Clustering

Clustering is done automatically in Payara Micro; when two instances of Payara Micro are started on the same network, they automatically cluster together, with absolutely no configuration needed.

---

If we don't want Payara Micro instances to join a cluster, we can start Payara Micro with the `--noCluster` command-line argument

---

Payara Micro (and Payara Server, for that matter) has an in-memory data grid used to share data across instances in a cluster. Payara's data grid is based on the popular open source Hazelcast in-memory data grid. For the most part, the data grid is transparent to us as application developers deploying applications to Payara Micro; however, it is used behind the scenes to implement Payara Micro specific clustering features, such as having application scoped CDI beans be shared across a cluster and allowing to fire CDI events to observer methods running on another instance of Payara Micro on the same cluster.

© David R. Heffelfinger 2022
D. R. Heffelfinger, *Payara Micro Revealed*, https://doi.org/10.1007/978-1-4842-8161-1_12

# Clustered Application Scoped CDI Beans

With Payara Micro, we can share the same instance of an application scoped bean across nodes in a network. To do so, all we have to do is annotate the application scoped bean with the @Clustered annotation, as illustrated in the following example.

```
package com.ensode.clusteredcdiappscopedbeans;

import fish.payara.cluster.Clustered;
//additional imports omitted

@Clustered
@ApplicationScoped
//Clustered application scoped bean must be serializable
public class DataCache implements Serializable {

  private Map<String, String> cachedValueMap = new HashMap<>();

  public void addMapEntry(String key, String value) {
    cachedValueMap.put(key, value);
  }

  public String retrieveValue(String key) {
    return cachedValueMap.get(key);
  }

  public Map<String, String> getCachedValueMap() {
    return cachedValueMap;
  }

  public void setCachedValueMap(Map<String, String> cachedValueMap) {
    this.cachedValueMap = cachedValueMap;
  }

}
```

A common use of application scoped CDI beans is to cache frequently used data so that we don't have to hit a database every time we need to retrieve it. With standard application scoped CDI beans, we would have to have a copy of the bean in each node of a cluster; keeping those instances in sync would not be a trivial task. With Payara's clustered CDI beans, there is a single instance shared across nodes.

As can be seen in the example, all we have to do to share an application scoped bean across nodes in a cluster is annotated with @Clustered and have it implement the Serializable interface; all the hard work to share the bean instance is done behind the scenes by Payara Micro.

---

Clustered application scoped CDI beans must be serializable; otherwise, our code will fail to deploy.

---

In order to use the @Clustered annotation, we need to add *payara-api* as a provided dependency to our application. When using Maven, we can do so by adding the appropriate dependency to the <dependencies> section of *pom.xml*.

```
<dependencyManagement>
  <dependencies>
    <dependency>
      <groupId>fish.payara.api</groupId>
      <artifactId>payara-bom</artifactId>
      <version>${version.payara}</version>
      <type>pom</type>
      <scope>import</scope>
    </dependency>
  </dependencies>
</dependencyManagement>

<dependencies>
  <dependency>
    <groupId>fish.payara.api</groupId>
    <artifactId>payara-api</artifactId>
    <scope>provided</scope>
  </dependency>
  <!-- additional dependencies omitted-->
</dependencies>
```

When using the Payara Maven Bill of Materials (BOM), dependency versions are specified in the BOM; therefore, we shouldn't specify them in our *pom.xml*.

To illustrate clustered application scoped CDI beans, we can write a simple RESTful web service that, in response to HTTP PUT and GET requests, adds or retrieves values to/from the Map in our clustered application scoped CDI bean.

```
package com.ensode.clusteredcdiappscopedbeans;

//imports omitted

@Path("cachedvalueaccessor")
public class CachedValueAccessorResource {

  @Inject
  private DataCache dataCache;

  @GET
  @Produces(MediaType.TEXT_PLAIN)
  public String getCachedValue(@QueryParam("key") String key) {
    return dataCache.retrieveValue(key);
  }

  @PUT
  @Consumes(MediaType.TEXT_PLAIN)
  public void addCachedValue(@QueryParam("key") String key,
    @QueryParam("value") String value) {
    dataCache.addMapEntry(key, value);
  }
}
```

Notice that there is nothing special we need to do to use our clustered application scoped CDI bean; we simply inject it via the @Inject annotation as usual.

At this point, we have a simple but complete example we can use to illustrate clustered application scoped CDI beans; we simply package our application in a WAR file and deploy it to two separate instances of Payara Micro, which will automatically form a cluster.

We can do so from the command line as follows:

```
java -jar path/to/payara-micro-5.2021.10.jar \
--contextroot clusteredapplicationbeansdemo --autoBindHttp \
--deploy target/clustered-application-beans-demo-1.0-SNAPSHOT.war
```

If we examine Payara Micro's output, we can see our application has been deployed and it is listening on the default 8080 HTTP port.

```
[2021-12-28T18:49:51.628-0500] [] [INFO] [] [PayaraMicro] [tid: _ThreadID=1
_ThreadName=main] [timeMillis: 1640735391628] [levelValue: 800] [[

Payara Micro URLs:
http://127.0.0.1:8080/clusteredapplicationbeansdemo

'clustered-application-beans-demo-1.0-SNAPSHOT' REST Endpoints:
GET /clusteredapplicationbeansdemo/webresources/application.wadl
GET /clusteredapplicationbeansdemo/webresources/cachedvalueaccessor
PUT /clusteredapplicationbeansdemo/webresources/cachedvalueaccessor

]]

[2021-12-28T18:49:51.629-0500] [] [INFO] [] [PayaraMicro] [tid: _ThreadID=1
_ThreadName=main] [timeMillis: 1640735391629] [levelValue: 800] Payara
Micro  5 #badassmicrofish (build 879) ready in 7,708 (ms)
```

We then use the same command on a different terminal window to deploy a second copy of our WAR file.

On the second instance of Payara Micro, we should see output similar to the following:

```
[2021-12-28T18:55:32.268-0500] [] [INFO] [] [PayaraMicro] [tid: _ThreadID=1
_ThreadName=main] [timeMillis: 1640735732268] [levelValue: 800] [[

Payara Micro URLs:
http://127.0.0.1:8081/clusteredapplicationbeansdemo

'clustered-application-beans-demo-1.0-SNAPSHOT' REST Endpoints:
GET /clusteredapplicationbeansdemo/webresources/application.wadl
GET /clusteredapplicationbeansdemo/webresources/cachedvalueaccessor
PUT /clusteredapplicationbeansdemo/webresources/cachedvalueaccessor

]]

[2021-12-28T18:55:32.268-0500] [] [INFO] [] [PayaraMicro] [tid: _ThreadID=1
_ThreadName=main] [timeMillis: 1640735732268] [levelValue: 800] Payara
Micro  5 #badassmicrofish (build 879) ready in 8,235 (ms)
```

Since we used the *--autoBindHttp* command-line argument for Payara Micro, the second instance listens for HTTP connections on the next available port (8081).

Additionally, there will be some output on the first instance of Payara Micro, which lets us know that the two instances formed a cluster; the output should look similar to the following:

```
[2021-12-28T18:55:28.239-0500] [] [INFO] [] [fish.payara.nucleus.cluster.
PayaraCluster] [tid: _ThreadID=55 _ThreadName=hz.wonderful_sutherland.
event-4] [timeMillis: 1640735728239] [levelValue: 800] Data Grid Instance
Added f3fc7680-1fec-4544-8d9e-b8e7d20c634b at Address /192.168.1.165:6901
```

```
[2021-12-28T18:55:28.242-0500] [] [INFO] [] [fish.payara.nucleus.cluster.
PayaraCluster] [tid: _ThreadID=55 _ThreadName=hz.wonderful_sutherland.
event-4] [timeMillis: 1640735728242] [levelValue: 800] [[
  Data Grid Status
Payara Data Grid State: DG Version: 4 DG Name: development DG Size: 2
Instances: {
 DataGrid: development Name: Magnanimous-Butterfish Lite: false This: true
 UUID: 730a2023-0f47-4822-b2d9-d905ffcd0505 Address: /192.168.1.165:6900
 DataGrid: development Lite: false This: false UUID:
 f3fc7680-1fec-4544-8d9e-b8e7d20c634b Address: /192.168.1.165:6901
}]]
```

---

Recall that Payara Micro's clustering capabilities are implemented via an in-memory data grid (Hazelcast); the output on the first instance of Payara Micro is letting us know that a data grid instance was added to the cluster.

---

If you refer to our example clustered application scoped CDI bean, you'll notice the map holding the cached data is initially empty; we can add an entry to it by sending an HTTP PUT request to either instance of Payara Micro in the cluster. For example, using curl to send an HTTP PUT request to the first instance:

```
$curl -XPUT 'http://localhost:8080/clusteredapplicationbeansdemo/
webresources/cachedvalueaccessor?key=foo&value=bar'
```

CHAPTER 12   PAYARA MICRO SPECIFIC FEATURES

At this point, we added an entry to the *Map* in the clustered application scoped CDI bean with a key of *foo* and a value of *bar*. Since the bean is clustered, the change is reflected across all nodes in the cluster.

We can now retrieve the value we just added by sending an HTTP GET request to either Payara Micro instance in the cluster; to make it interesting, let's send an HTTP GET request to the second instance in the cluster to retrieve the value we just added on the first instance:

```
$ curl http://localhost:8081/clusteredapplicationbeansdemo/webresources/
cachedvalueaccessor?key=foo
bar
```

The text below the curl command is the response from the second instance; as we can see, we got the expected value, which was set by sending an HTTP PUT request to the first instance in the cluster.

# Remote CDI Events

With Payara Micro, CDI events can be observed across the network by applications deployed in a different node from the application firing the event. To fire a remote CDI event, we need to annotate the event being fired with @Outbound and the parameter in the method handling the event with @Inbound. The following example illustrates how to fire a remote event; it is a modified version of the CDI events example we saw in Chapter 4, updated to fire remote CDI events.

```
package com.ensode.cdievents;

import com.ensode.cdievents.qualifier.Deleted;
import com.ensode.cdievents.qualifier.Updated;
import fish.payara.micro.cdi.Outbound;

@Path("countryservice")
public class CountryService {

  @Inject
  private @Updated @Outbound
  Event<Country> countryEvent;
```

211

```
@Inject
private @Deleted @Outbound
Event<Country> countryDeletedEvent;

@Inject
private CountryLookup countryLookup;

@GET
@Produces(MediaType.APPLICATION_JSON)
public Country handleGetRequest(@QueryParam("countryAbbrev") String
countryAbbrev) {
  return countryLookup.getCountry(countryAbbrev);
}

@PUT
@Consumes(MediaType.APPLICATION_JSON)
public void updateCountry(Country country) {
  countryEvent.fire(country);
}

@DELETE
@Consumes(MediaType.APPLICATION_JSON)
public void deleteCountry(@QueryParam("countryAbbrev") String
countryAbbrev) {
  Country country=countryLookup.getCountry(countryAbbrev);
  countryDeletedEvent.fire(country);
}

}
```

The preceding RESTful web service code fires two types of country events: one when a country is updated and another when a country is deleted. Recall from Chapter 4 that we can use qualifiers to distinguish between events of the same type; in our example, the @Updated and @Deleted qualifiers are used to distinguish between these two events. In addition to our custom @Updated and @Deleted qualifiers, we annotated both events with the Payara-provided @Outbound qualifier; this qualifier is used to fire the event across the network so that event observer methods in other nodes can handle it. As a matter of fact, the only thing we have to do to convert a standard CDI event into a remote CDI event is to annotate the Event instance declaration with @Outbound.

For this example, we refactored the application so that the event observer is deployed in a separate WAR file; this way, we can deploy the observer to a different instance of Payara Micro.

Just like in Chapter 4, we have three observer methods across two different Java classes; we have a CountryManager class that has two observer methods: one for country events annotated with @Updated and another one for events annotated with @Deleted.

```java
package com.ensode.cdi.remote.event.observer;

import com.ensode.cdievents.Country;
import com.ensode.cdievents.CountryLookup;
import com.ensode.cdievents.qualifier.Deleted;
import com.ensode.cdievents.qualifier.Updated;
import fish.payara.micro.cdi.Inbound;
//additional imports omitted

@ApplicationScoped
public class CountryManager {

  private static final Logger LOGGER =
    Logger.getLogger(CountryManager.class.getName());

  @Inject
  private CountryLookup countryLookup;

  public void updateCountry(
    @Observes @Inbound @Updated Country country) {
    LOGGER.log(Level.INFO, String.format(
      "Updating the following country: %s", country.getName()));
    countryLookup.updateCountry(country);
  }

  public void deleteCountry(
    @Observes @Inbound @Deleted Country country) {
    LOGGER.log(Level.INFO, String.format(
    "Deleting the following country: %s", country.getName()));
    countryLookup.deleteCountry(country);
  }
}
```

The only difference between this example and the corresponding example in Chapter 4 is the addition of the @Inbound annotation to the observer method parameter, which is needed to handle events fired across the network.

We have an additional class with an observer method; it listens for any country event (i.e., no custom qualifiers like @Updated or @Deleted are used) and simply sends output to the log on the observer method.

```
package com.ensode.cdi.remote.event.observer;

import com.ensode.cdievents.Country;
import fish.payara.micro.cdi.Inbound;
//additional imports omitted

@ApplicationScoped
public class CountryEventLogger {

  private static final Logger LOGGER = Logger.getLogger(CountryEvent
  Logger.class.getName());

  public void logCountryEvent(
    @Observes @Inbound Country country) {
    LOGGER.log(Level.INFO, String.format(
      "Event fired for the following country: %s",
        country.getName()));
  }

}
```

Unsurprisingly, all we had to do to have this observer method listen for remote events is to annotate its parameter with the @Inbound annotation.

At this point, we are ready to test our refactored CDI event code; we deploy the WAR file containing the code to fire the events to an instance of Payara Micro listening on HTTP port 8080. Payara Micro's output lets us know the endpoints we can use to send HTTP requests to our RESTful web service.

```
Payara Micro URLs:
http://127.0.0.1:8080/cdi-remote-events

'cdi-remote-events-1.0-SNAPSHOT' REST Endpoints:
GET    /cdi-remote-events/webresources/application.wadl
```

```
DELETE  /cdi-remote-events/webresources/countryservice
GET     /cdi-remote-events/webresources/countryservice
PUT     /cdi-remote-events/webresources/countryservice

]]
```

We then deploy the second WAR file containing event observers to a second instance of Payara Micro listening on port 8081.

```
[2021-12-29T18:54:07.730-0500] [] [INFO] [] [PayaraMicro] [tid: _ThreadID=1
_ThreadName=main] [timeMillis: 1640822047730] [levelValue: 800] [[

Payara Micro URLs:
http://127.0.0.1:8081/cdi-remote-events-observer

]]
```

Since we didn't package any RESTful web services in the second WAR file (only CDI beans), no endpoints are displayed on the output of the second Payara Micro instance.

At this point, we are ready to test our code; we can send an HTTP DELETE request to the first Payara Micro instance, which will cause it to fire a remote CDI event; we can do so via a curl command as follows:

*$ curl -XDELETE http://localhost:8080/cdi-remote-events/webresources/countryservice?countryAbbrev=AU*

At this point, if we inspect the output of Payara Micro, we should see the log entries added by the appropriate CDI remote event observer methods.

```
[2021-12-29T18:59:21.152-0500] [] [INFO] [] [com.ensode.cdi.remote.event.
observer.CountryEventLogger] [tid: _ThreadID=121 _ThreadName=concurrent/__
defaultManagedExecutorService-managedThreadFactory-Thread-9] [timeMillis:
1640822361152] [levelValue: 800] Event fired for the following country:
Australia

[2021-12-29T18:59:21.156-0500] [] [INFO] [] [com.ensode.cdi.remote.event.
observer.CountryManager] [tid: _ThreadID=121 _ThreadName=concurrent/__
defaultManagedExecutorService-managedThreadFactory-Thread-9] [timeMillis:
1640822361156] [levelValue: 800] Deleting the following country: Australia
```

As illustrated by our example, firing remote CDI events in Payara Micro takes very little work on our part; we simply annotate the event to be fired with `@Outbound` and the corresponding event observer method parameters with `@Inbound`; all the hard work is done by Payara Micro and is transparent to us as application developers.

# Uber Jars

Uber Jars are executable JAR files that bundle both our application code and the Payara Micro runtime. Creating an Uber Jar can potentially simplify executing our applications; all we have to do is run the executable WAR file, without having to pass any arguments to Payara Micro.

# Creating Uber Jars

We can create an Uber Jar by passing the *--outputUberJar* command-line option to Payara Micro, as in the following example:

```
java -jar path/to/payara-micro/5.2021.10/payara-micro-5.2021.10.
jar --deploy target/cdi-remote-events-1.0-SNAPSHOT.war --autoBindHttp
--outputUberJar cdiremoteevents.jar
```

The *--outputUberJar* command-line option takes an argument specifying the name of the JAR file to be created.

Most command-line arguments we pass to Payara Micro are recorded so that they don't need to be specified when executing the JAR file; in our example, the generated JAR file will execute Payara Micro with the *--autoBindHttp* option enabled by default. One notable exception is that the `--contextRoot` command-line argument is not recorded; the context root of the generated JAR file will always be the name of the deployed WAR file (*cdi-remote-events-1.0-SNAPSHOT.war* in our example).

The preceding command generates a JAR file with the name we specified in the current directory; to execute it, we simply run the same way we run any executable JAR file:

```
java -jar cdiremoteevents.jar
```

We should see Payara Micro's usual output on the terminal window:

```
[2021-12-31T09:30:37.148-0500] [] [INFO] [] [PayaraMicro] [tid: _ThreadID=1
_ThreadName=main] [timeMillis: 1640961037148] [levelValue: 800] [[

Payara Micro URLs:
http://192.168.1.165:8080/cdi-remote-events-1.0-SNAPSHOT

'cdi-remote-events-1.0-SNAPSHOT' REST Endpoints:
GET     /cdi-remote-events-1.0-SNAPSHOT/webresources/application.wadl
DELETE /cdi-remote-events-1.0-SNAPSHOT/webresources/countryservice
GET     /cdi-remote-events-1.0-SNAPSHOT/webresources/countryservice
PUT     /cdi-remote-events-1.0-SNAPSHOT/webresources/countryservice

]]

[2021-12-31T09:30:37.148-0500] [] [INFO] [] [PayaraMicro] [tid: _ThreadID=1
_ThreadName=main] [timeMillis: 1640961037148] [levelValue: 800] Payara
Micro  5 #badassmicrofish (build 879) ready in 8,995 (ms)
```

If we wish to change the context root, we can rename the WAR file to have the context root name we want; for example, renaming *cdi-remote-events-1.0-SNAPSHOT. war* to *cdiremoteevents.war* will result in the application having a context root of */ cdiremoteevents*.

# Embedding Payara Micro

We can embed Payara Micro inside other Java applications. Doing so allows us to start/ stop/deploy apps, etc., programmatically via Payara Micro's Java API. The following example illustrates how to do this:

```java
package com.ensode.embeddedpayaramicroexample;

import fish.payara.micro.BootstrapException;
import fish.payara.micro.PayaraMicro;
import java.io.File;

public class Main {
```

```
public void startPayaraMicro() throws BootstrapException {
  File warFile = new File("/path/to/some.war");
  PayaraMicro.getInstance().
    setHttpAutoBind(true).
    bootStrap().deploy("applicationname",
      "contextroot", warFile);
}

public static void main(String[] args)
  throws BootstrapException {
  new Main().startPayaraMicro();
}

}
```

The PayaraMicro class is a singleton; it has a static getInstance() method that returns the PayaraMicro instance; we can configure Payara Micro programmatically by invoking setter and getter methods; for instance, in our example, we are invoking setHttpAutoBind(true), which is equivalent to passing the --*autoBind* command-line argument to Payara Micro when running from the command line. The API to configure Payara Micro is very intuitive for those familiar with running Payara Micro from the command line; refer to the official Payara Micro API JavaDoc at https://javadoc. io/doc/fish.payara.extras/payara-micro/latest/index.html; of particular interest is the fish.payara.micro package, particularly the PayaraMicro class and the PayaraMicroRuntime interface.

Once we have configured the embedded Payara Micro instance, we invoke its bootstrap() method, which returns an implementation of the PayaraMicroRuntime interface; to deploy our WAR file, we invoke its deploy() method, which takes three arguments: a String defining a name for our application, a second String defining the context root for the WAR file, and an instance of java.io.File representing our WAR file.

We can then run our application like any other stand-alone Java application. For Maven projects, the easiest way is to use the Exec Maven plug-in, which automatically sets the class path from our project dependencies; for example:

*mvn exec:java -Dexec.mainClass="com.ensode.embeddedpayaramicroexample.Main"*

would run our application, which in turn would start a Payara Micro instance; we can then send HTTP requests to this Payara Micro instance as usual.

# Summary

In this chapter, we covered Payara Micro features that go beyond the Jakarta EE and MicroProfile standards. We explained how Payara Micro instances cluster automatically. We also covered how to share application scoped CDI beans across cluster nodes, as well as how to send CDI events across the network to listeners deployed to other Payara Micro instances on the cluster.

Additionally, we covered how to create so-called Uber Jars, which are executable JAR files that contain both our application code and the Payara Micro runtime bundled together, allowing us to run Payara Micro and deploy our code by running an executable JAR file.

We then covered how to embed Payara Micro in our Java applications and how we can configure and deploy our applications and start Payara Micro programmatically.

# CHAPTER 13

# Payara Cloud

Typically, deploying an application to the cloud involves a lot more work than "just" developing the application; "pods" (typically stripped-down virtual Linux servers) may need to be configured to run our application; there may be complex configuration files that may need to be developed before our application can run properly.

Having to perform all of these administration tasks is where the popular *DevOps* term came from, where software developers are now responsible for tasks that were traditionally performed by system administrators. These tasks frequently fall beyond typical software developers' areas of expertise; it is not uncommon for a development team to have to go through a "trial by fire" period when initially migrating their applications to the cloud, having to quickly learn all of these additional administration tasks now needed to successfully deploy the application.

Payara Cloud provides a Payara Micro instance in the cloud and automatically performs all the necessary configuration; all that is needed is to deploy a standard WAR file; all configuration is generated automatically, akin to deploying to a more traditional "heavyweight" Jakarta EE application server.

## Signing Up for Payara Cloud

To sign up to Payara Cloud, visit the following URL: `https://payara.cloud/#subscribe`.

---

At the time of writing, Payara Cloud is not yet open to the public; the fine folks at Payara allowed us to preview Payara Cloud so that we could write about it in the book. Thanks Rudy De Busscher, Payara Product Manager and Developer Advocate, as well as the Payara Marketing Team!

---

© David R. Heffelfinger 2022
D. R. Heffelfinger, *Payara Micro Revealed*, https://doi.org/10.1007/978-1-4842-8161-1_13

There are three plans available, to fit your budget and needs. There are Basic, Standard, and Premium plans, each providing additional computing resources such as CPU and RAM and levels of support. Visit the preceding URL for details on each plan.

# Developing Applications for Payara Cloud

Developing applications to be deployed in Payara Cloud takes no additional effort than developing applications to a local Payara Micro instance. If your application deploys and runs well in Payara Micro, it will deploy and run well when deployed to Payara Cloud.

# Deploying Applications to Payara Cloud

Payara Cloud has a concept of *namespaces*; a namespace is a group of related applications.

Before you can upload an application to Payara Cloud for the first time, you need to create a namespace.

## Creating a Namespace

A namespace can be created by clicking on the *Create New Namespace* button at the top right of the welcome screen of the Payara Cloud web-based interface, as illustrated in Figure 13-1.

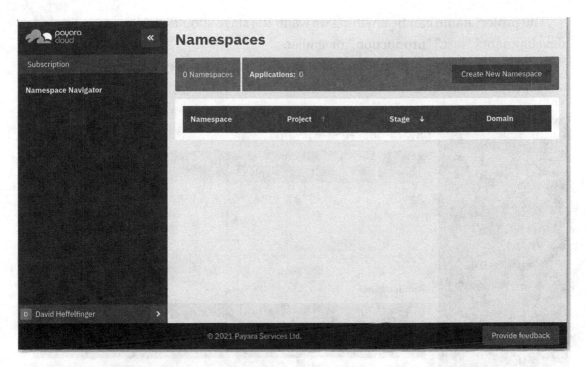

**Figure 13-1.** *Creating a namespace*

When creating a namespace, we need to enter a *Project* name and *Stage*, as illustrated in Figure 13-2.

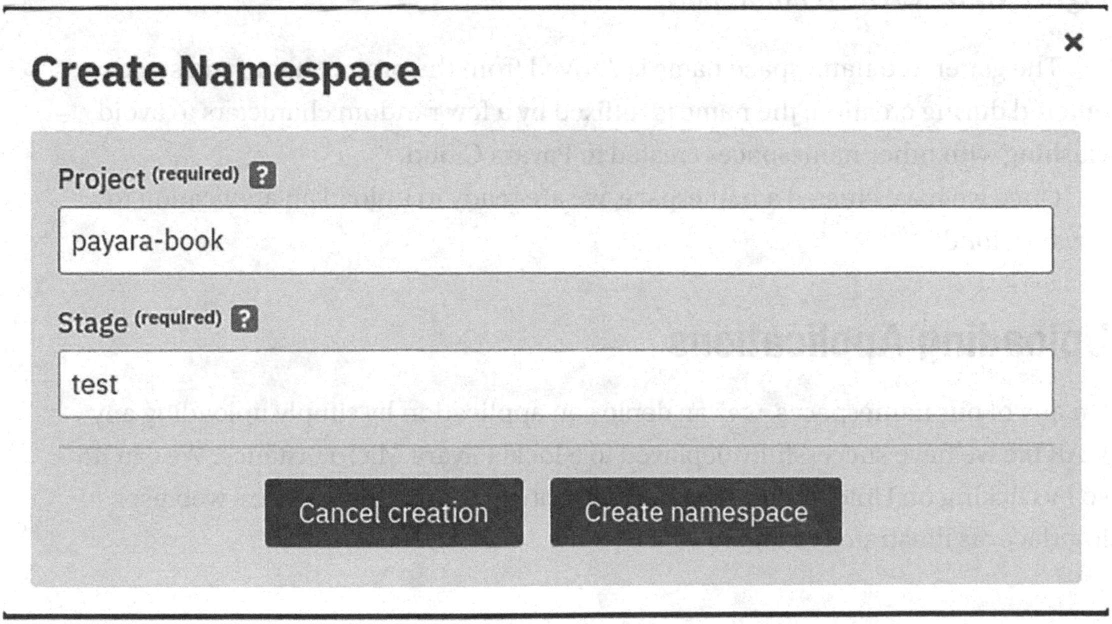

# Create Namespace ✕

**Project** (required) ❓

payara-book

**Stage** (required) ❓

test

Cancel creation          Create namespace

**Figure 13-2.** *Namespace project and stage*

223

The project name can be anything we want; the stage should be something like "development," "test," "production," or similar.

After entering our project name and stage, we click on *Create namespace*, and our namespace is created, as illustrated in Figure 13-3.

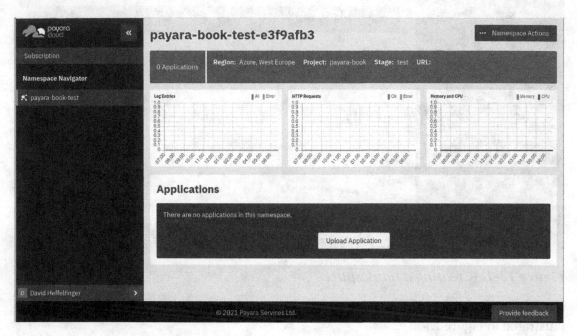

***Figure 13-3.*** *Created namespace*

The generated namespace name is derived from the project name and stage we entered during creation; the name is suffixed by a few random characters to avoid clashing with other namespaces created in Payara Cloud.

Once we have created a namespace, we are ready to upload an application to Payara Cloud.

# Uploading Applications

On any of our namespaces, we can deploy an application by simply uploading any WAR file we have successfully deployed to a local Payara Micro instance. We can do so by clicking on Upload Application at the bottom of our namespace's web user interface, as illustrated in Figure 13-4.

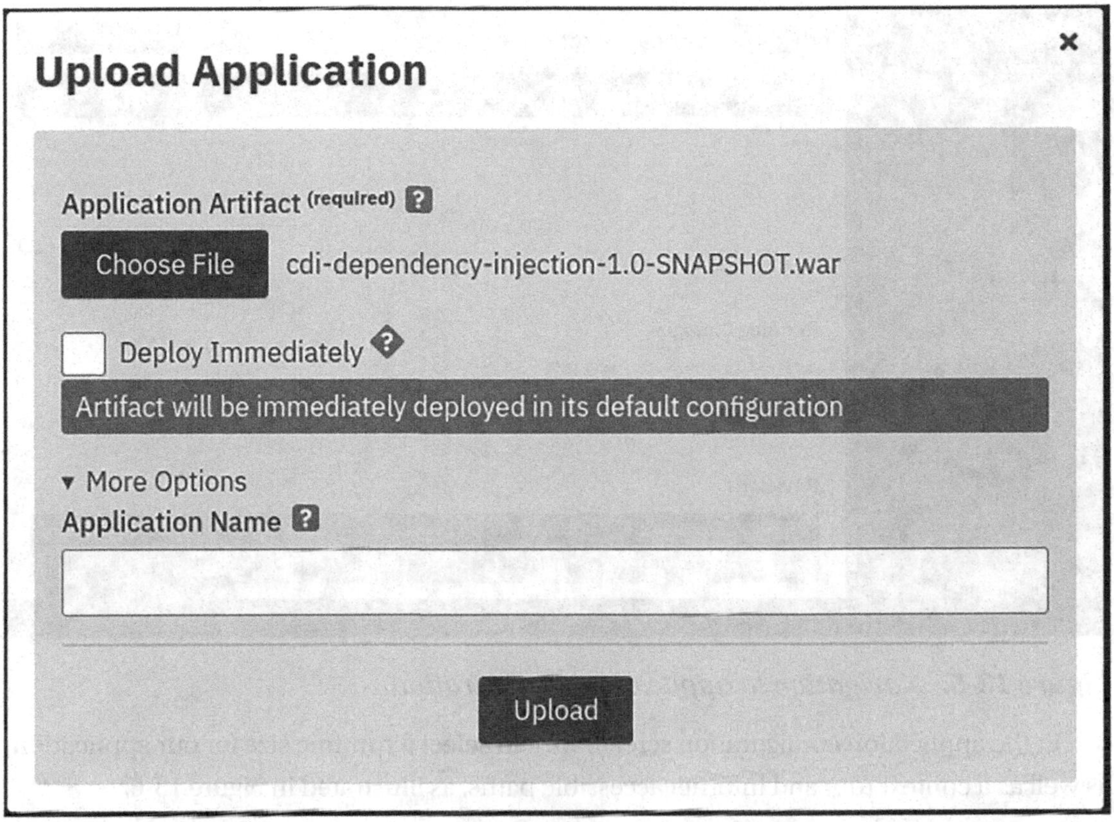

*Figure 13-4.* *Uploading an application to Payara Cloud*

If we check *Deploy Immediately*, the application will be immediately deployed using a default configuration; if we leave it unchecked, we will need to configure and deploy the application ourselves.

We can give our application a name; if the application was built with Maven, Payara Cloud will use the artifact ID of our WAR file as the application name by default; if this is the behavior we want, then we don't need to specify an application name.

If we did not deploy our application immediately, the application will have a status of *Configured* right after we upload it; we can edit the application's default configuration by clicking on *Revision Actions* and then on *Edit Configuration* as illustrated in Figure 13-5.

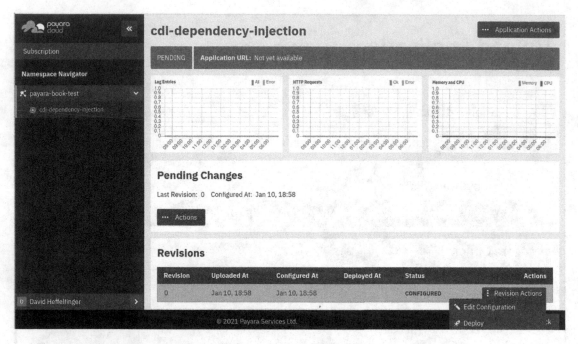

**Figure 13-5.** *Navigation to application configuration*

In the application configuration screen, we can select a runtime size for our application, as well as a context root and Internet accessible paths, as illustrated in Figure 13-6.

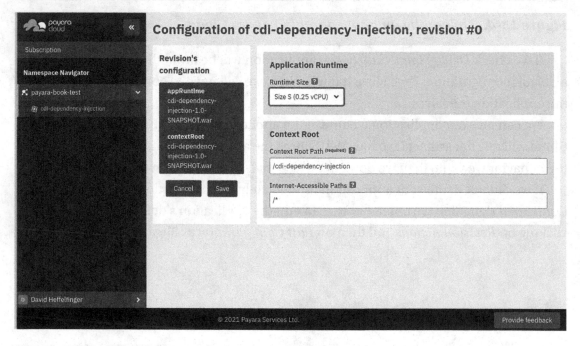

**Figure 13-6.** *Modifying application configuration*

By default, all paths in our application are exposed to the Internet; if we wish to expose only certain RESTful web service endpoints or pages to the Internet, we can specify space-separated paths in the *Internet-Accessible Paths* field; for example, if we only wanted paths starting with /public or /default to be Internet accessible, we would enter the following value to that field:

```
/public* /default*
```

For our example, it is fine to have all paths Internet accessible; therefore, we can accept the default /* value, which allows this.

We can save our configuration by clicking *Save*.

At this point, our application is still in *Configured* status; we need to deploy it by clicking on *Revision Actions*, followed by *Deploy*.

After a few seconds, our application status changes to *Deployed*, as illustrated in Figure 13-7.

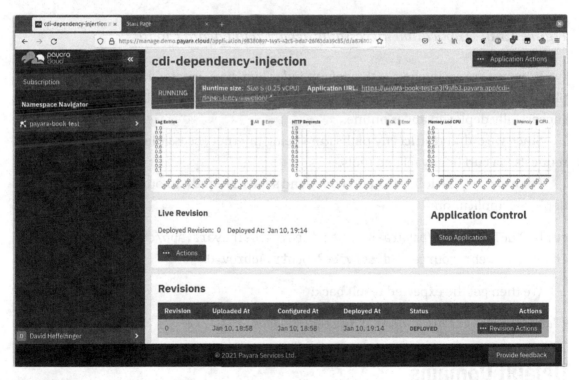

***Figure 13-7.***  *Deployed application*

At this point, our application is live; we can see its URL at the top right of the Payara Cloud application management console.

# Running Applications in Payara Cloud

Now that our application is deployed, we can simply click on the URL displayed at the top right of the Payara Cloud application management console; we can see the default index. html page displayed on our browser, served by Payara Cloud, as illustrated in Figure 13-8.

*Figure 13-8.* *Application successfully deployed to Payara Cloud*

What we are seeing here is the default *index.html* page created by the Payara Maven plug-in; it won't win any web design contests, but it proves our application has been successfully deployed and is online.

Since we didn't restrict any paths from being Internet accessible, we can send HTTP requests via curl or any related tools.

For example, the following curl command sends a request to our Payara Cloud deployed application:

```
curl -XGET https://payara-book-test-e3f9afb3.payara.app/cdi-dependency-
injection/webresources/cdiservice?countryAbbrev=UK
```

We then get the expected result back:

```
{"abbreviation":"UK","name":"United Kingdom"}
```

# Default Domains

As we can see from our examples above, the generated domain name (`https://payarabook-test-e3f9afb3.payara.app` in our example) is not very pretty or memorable; it will serve our purposes just fine for development or testing purposes;

however, for production, we probably want to provide our user with a nice, easy-to-remember domain name. Payara Cloud Standard and Premium plans allow us to define a custom domain name.

## Custom Domains

To create a custom domain name, click on *Namespace Actions* at the top right of the Payara Cloud namespace management console and then click on *Custom Domain*, as illustrated in Figure 13-9.

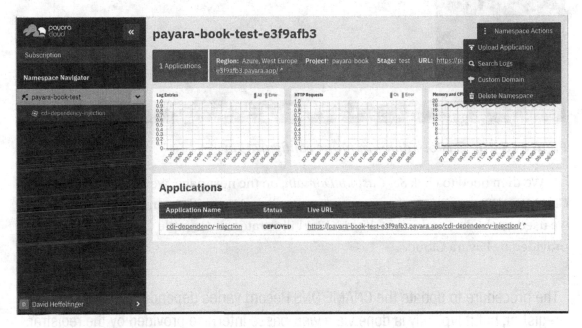

***Figure 13-9.*** *Navigating to custom domain name configuration*

We then specify our custom domain in the *Custom Domain Name* field as illustrated in Figure 13-10; the domain name must be a valid domain we have registered with a domain registrar.

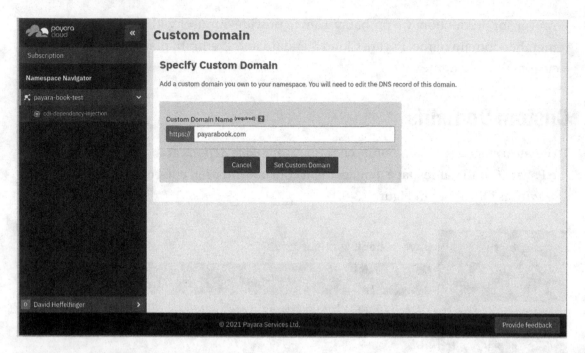

***Figure 13-10.*** *Custom domain name configuration*

We then need to click *Set Custom Domain*; on the next page, we are provided with a CNAME DNS record we can use to update our domain with the domain name registrar we used to obtain our domain. Figure 13-11 illustrates an example CNAME DNS Record provided by Payara Cloud.

---

The procedure to update the CNAME DNS Record varies depending on the domain registrar, but it typically is done via a web-based interface provided by the registrar.

---

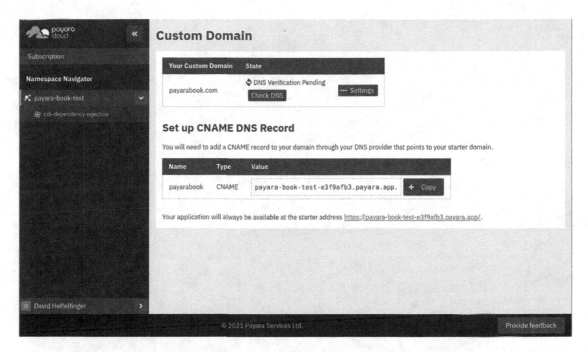

*Figure 13-11.* *CNAME DNS Record configuration*

Once we have updated the CNAME DNS Record, we can click on Check DNS to make sure it was set up correctly. If that was the case, we can now use our custom domain to access our application.

# Summary

In this chapter, we provided an introduction to Payara Cloud and how it can be used to deploy applications to the cloud without needing to update complex configuration files.

We covered how to sign up to Payara Cloud and how any application that deploys successfully against Payara Micro can be deployed to Payara Cloud.

We also covered how to configure applications deployed to Payara Cloud, including how to set up the runtime size, how to set the context root, and how to hide paths from the Internet, if necessary.

Additionally, we covered how to access our applications after they have been successfully deployed to Payara Cloud.

Finally, we covered how to use custom domains for our Payara Cloud applications.

# Index

## A

Application metrics
   attributes, 106
   @ConcurrentGauge, 109, 110
   @Counted annotation, 107
   Counter interface, 115
   @Gauge, 108, 109
   @Metered, 110–112
   programmatic metrics, 116–119
   @SimplyTimed, 114, 115
   @Timed, 111–113
Asynchronous
   client interface methods, 122, 123
   CompletionStage interfaces, 121
   endpoint, 122
   invoked methods, 124
   RESTful web service endpoints, 121
Automatic clustering, *see* Clustering

## B

Bill of Materials (BOM), 9–10, 168, 207

## C

Cloud application, 221
   deployment
      concepts, 222
      modification, 226
      namespace creation, 222–224
      navigation, 226
      upload application, 224–227

development, 222
   running application
      browser window, 228
      curl command, 228
      custom domain name, 229–231
      default domains, 228
      index.html page, 228
      record configuration, 231
   singing up, 221
Clustering
   Bill of Materials (BOM), 207
   command line, 208
   data grid, 205
   fire remote CDI events, 211–216
   HTTP requests, 214
   observer method, 214
   *pom.xml* file, 207
   scoped bean, 206–211
   Uber Jars, 216, 217
   WAR file, 209, 215
Configuration sources
   abstract methods, 89
   cloud provider, 88
   converters
      getCustomer() method, 99
      numeric types, 95, 96
      Payara Micro, 96
      properties, 98
      registration directory tree, 98–101
   custom configuration, 89–92
   directory tree, 92
   dynamic properties, 92–95

© David R. Heffelfinger 2022
D. R. Heffelfinger, *Payara Micro Revealed*, https://doi.org/10.1007/978-1-4842-8161-1

Printed in the United States
by Baker & Taylor Publisher Services

Printed in the United States
by Baker & Taylor Publisher Services